ARCHITECTURAL BIRDHOUSES

ARCHITECTURAL BIRDHOUSES

15 Famous Buildings to Make for Your Feathered Friends

Thomas Stender

Main Street
A Division of Sterling Publishing Co., Inc.
New York

DEDICATION

To my mother and father,
who have always fed me,
and always fed the birds.

They gave me the
swell jig saw in the photos,
and they still feed the birds.

CHRIS BRYANT
Art direction
Production

ANDY RAE
Woodworking editor

EVAN BRACKEN
Project photography

THOMAS STENDER
How-to photography
Illustrations

VERONIKA ALICE GUNTER
RAIN NEWCOMB
Editorial assistants

Library of Congress Cataloging-in-Publication Data Available

10 9 8 7 6 5 4 3 2 1

Published by Lark Books, a division of
Sterling Publishing Co., Inc.
387 Park Avenue South, New York, NY 10016

Distributed in Canada by Sterling Publishing
c/o Canadian Manda Group, One Atlantic Avenue, Suite 105
Toronto, Ontario, Canada M6K 3E7

Distributed in Australia by Capricorn Link (Australia) Pty. Ltd.
P.O. Box 704, Windsor, NSW 2756, Australia

Distributed in the U.K. by:
Guild of Master Craftsman Publications Ltd.
Castle Place 166 High Street, Lewes, East Sussex, England BN7 1XU
Tel: (+44) 1273 477374 Fax (+44) 1273 478606
Email: pubs@thegmcgroup.com, Web: www.gmcpublications.com

Every effort has been made to ensure that all the information in this book is accurate. However, due to differing conditions, tools, and individual skills, the publisher cannot be responsible for any injuries, losses, or other damages that may result from the use of the information in this book.

If you have questions or comments about this book, please contact:
Lark Books, 67 Broadway, Asheville, NC 28801, (828) 253-0467

Printed in China

Sterling 1-4027-1140-9

CONTENTS

INTRODUCTION

BUILDING BIRDHOUSES PROVIDES A LOT OF PLEASURE. There's the building process itself, which gratifies our desire to make a beautiful and functional object. And we clearly find birdhouses, in particular, attractive: some people are avid birdhouse collectors, and others use them to decorate their homes. Finally, they afford us the opportunity to provide safe habitats in which wild birds can raise their families. Creativity, aesthetic gratification, and nurturance—what more could you ask? But the projects that follow add one more pleasure, because each is an architectural miniature, evoking an important building or a popular house style.

The birdhouse designs in this book violate one of the first rules of architectural practice, that the building should reflect the client (in this case, the birds). I admit that these designs are entirely human buildings scaled and adapted for birds. In fact, they put the builder ahead of the client. I hope you find them charming, and I trust that the instructions will help you through any construction thickets you haven't encountered before. I've taken care of the blueprints and the building permits; siting, erection, and final inspection are up to you.

I taught myself woodworking by copying antique furniture from pictures in books. I soon found that the original furniture makers were teaching me about design at the same time. Struggling with curves and proportions forced me to look closer, ferreting out their interior logic. When I successfully reproduced a certain shape or line, it showed me its rightness, both in its relationship with the whole design and in the way the wood and tools allowed me to form it. Designing these birdhouses brought similar revelations, as I saw reasons and details I hadn't noticed before, even in buildings which were familiar. Drawing the Farnsworth House Birdfeeder, for instance, revealed just how extended are the proportions of the actual Farnsworth House. All of which is to say that I can offer you two justifications for the designs presented here: they make us look more closely at the original buildings, and they're just plain cute.

But they're also real birdhouses. While some of you will want to build these projects as interior decoration, all of them have been designed to accommodate particular bird families. Some of them are adaptable to other species. Consult the table on page 137 to find other birds with similar housing requirements, and change the dimensions of your chosen design accordingly. The extent of the alterations you'll have to make depends on the design, so read the instructions and the drawings until you understand the relationships of its various parts. Then you can mount your house in a likely spot (see Mounting and Maintenence, page 140), and enjoy watching your new neighbors.

So choose your birdhouse, and start building! But please be careful. Woodworking involves tools that don't care a bit about the well-being of your hands. Pay attention to what you're doing and where your various body parts are now—and where they're likely to be next. Push sticks hurt a lot less than fingers if they slip. Don't try to exceed your own capabilities or those of your tools. For instance, don't attempt to manhandle a whole sheet of plywood past the table-saw blade to cut the little piece you need. Use a circular saw to cut off a reasonably-sized piece instead, one from which you can cut several of the pieces the project requires. Then you can comfortably cut them to size on the table saw. Finally, make sure that your tools stay sharp. Sharp tools require less force to do their job, so you're more likely to stay in control, which is what good, safe woodworking is about.

TOOLS AND TIPS

STATIONARY POWER TOOLS

Woodworkers love to talk about tools, so let's start there. In the projects that follow, I suggest particular tools because I believe that each is best for the job at hand. There are almost always alternatives, and often I list those, too. I also explain why I've chosen a tool when the reason may not be obvious. But don't let the lack of a tool deter you from tackling a project you'd like to build. If you're tenacious, and willing to learn the skills involved, you can build all these birdhouses with hand tools alone. More likely, you'll improvise, as woodworkers always have, making do with the power tools you own, and using a machine in your neighbor's shop when necessary.

But be careful: When you're inventively extending the usefulness of one of your machines, don't exceed its capabilities or your own. In many instances, especially with small workpieces, you can get the job done more efficiently and more safely with hand tools. To take an outrageous example, one of the last steps in building the Gothic Cathedral Pileated Woodpecker House (see page 114) involves gluing thin pieces of pine across the front of the cathedral. I suggest attaching overlength strips and trimming them to length afterwards with a handsaw. It would be possible to trim those strips on the table saw, but you wouldn't think of doing such a thing, would you? And yet, in moments of narrow insanity, we've all considered trying something equally wacky. That's the time for a walk around the block, expanding one's vision and considering the alternatives.

If you get an itch to buy new tools before starting a new project (and I know you do), consider this: Instead of going for the glitzy, big tool that promises to solve all your woodworking and personal problems, make sure you have the plain tools that actually do make the work go more smoothly. You need a flat, sturdy work surface, for instance. And clamps in a variety of types and sizes. A good woodworking vise, an accurate square, quality chisels capable of holding an edge, a low-angle block plane—these simple tools give more value for the money by making your work easier, more accurate, and more pleasurable. I'll tell you a secret. Within the past year, I bought a tool that I can't believe I'd done without, that has changed my working habits and given me many little moments of joy. It's an electric pencil sharpener.

But since you ask, here's a list of the stationary power tools I used in building the projects in this book:

Table saw
Band saw
Drill press
Jointer
Thickness planer
Router mounted in a router table

Of these, I consider only the table saw really crucial, because it does several things more accurately than I can accomplish in any other way. Some of you may be surprised at the omission of a radial-arm saw from the list. While it's great for house-framing and other jobs that involve cutting long pieces of wood, a radial arm saw can't achieve the accuracy of a table saw, nor can it rip and bevel as safely. In nearly all the projects, a jigsaw can easily substitute for the band saw. However, I would want access to a band saw for the Duomo Double Finch House (see page 127).

PHOTO 1

PHOTO 2

PHOTO 3

MITER GAUGE STOP

Commonly used on table saws and radial-arm saws, a stop allows us to cut to the same length repeatedly. The handiest kind of stop is a drop stop, which attaches to the miter gauge so that it adjusts laterally, and is hinged so that it can flip out of the way when we don't need it. If a drop stop came with your miter gauge, you're all set. If one is available for your miter gauge, go buy it now. If not, you can achieve the same results by clamping a scrap to your miter gauge fence. Better yet, spend a few minutes to make a drop stop from two blocks of wood and a hinge. Make one of the blocks longer so that you can clamp it to your miter gauge. Then you're ready for efficient fun: Cut a square end on every board from which you intend to cut pieces of the same length, drop or clamp the stop in place, and start sawing, placing each squared end against the stop. (See photo 1.)

I often use the stop even when I have only one cut to make because I can measure directly from the stop to the blade, eliminating the step of marking the edge of the board. In addition, by setting the drop stop first and flipping it out of the way to square the first end, I can turn on the table saw once to make both cuts.

Use a stop whenever you make miter cuts, too. The stop will prevent your workpiece from slipping away from the blade during the cut. If you need to cut opposing miters, as for a frame, or the friezes and architraves in the Doric Temple Robin House (see page 42), make the first miter cut using the stop. (See photo 2.) Then put the cutoff from your first miter against the stop, adjust the length, and cut the rest of the pieces, as shown in photo 3. (If you have a simple, clamp-on stop, you should cut one end of all the peices first, then adjust the stop for length.)

You can extend the usefulness of the stop for making incremental cuts, such as a series of equally-spaced dados, by making a set of identical blocks, each the length of the interval of the cuts. Put one block against the stop to make a second cut, say 1" away from the first. Add another block to cut 2" away. You get the idea.

BAND SAW TIPS

A narrow blade cuts tight curves best, of course. For instance, I used a ¼" blade for the buttresses on the Gothic Cathedral Pileated Woodpecker House (see photo 4 and page 114). For most work, however, I use a ½" hook-tooth blade with three teeth per inch. This blade cuts freely and has enough set to saw most curves, even though I sometimes have to back up and widen the kerf. But sawing curves is easy; the difficulty comes in sawing straighter lines on the band saw. Here's how to get better control: use the back of the blade as a moving, miniature rip fence. Angle your workpiece just enough so that one edge of the kerf contacts the back edge of the blade. Now you can "lean" gently against the blade while you cut, eliminating the wandering tendencies of a straight band saw cut.

PHOTO 4

PHOTO 5

MY FAVORITE TOOLS

I don't know how you can get along without these: a low-angle block plane, a dozuki saw, and a clear plastic 18" ruler. (See photo 5.) While it doesn't plane long grain as cleanly as a larger smooth plane, the low-angle block plane does a reasonable job with most woods, and, most important, it cuts end grain very well. Small enough to use with one hand, narrow enough to plane slightly concave surfaces, it's near my work all the time.

A dozuki is a fine-toothed Japanese backsaw which, like all Japanese saws, cuts on the pull stroke. Because of that, the blade (and its kerf) can be much thinner than Western saws, making it perfect for flush-trimming. The dozuki I use has a replaceable blade, with two blade options available. The coarser one (still plenty fine) works well for general small cutting, and the finer blade is great for dovetails and other precision work.

Even if you have a passel of rulers, get yourself a clear, flexible plastic ruler marked for centering, with lines in ⅛" increments across its width. Then use it to find centers, to draw parallel lines, and on and on. It's inexpensive at art- and office-supply stores.

One final tool tip: You can learn a lot about woodworking, as well as about tools, from fine tool catalogs. Look for the ads in quality woodworking magazines and send for a few mail-order catalogs. You'll find tools you've never heard of, and tools that suggest better ways of working. At the very least, you'll widen your range of tool choices beyond those available in your local hardware store.

BORING ENTRANCE HOLES

Almost every project in this book requires boring a fairly large entrance hole. Use a drill press for these holes, always put a scrap piece of plywood under your workpiece, and clamp the workpiece to the drill press table. You can use several kinds of bits to make these holes, but Forstner bits work best in plywood for holes up to 2" in diameter. (See photo 6.) The thin, face veneer on many plywoods tears easily, and Forstner bits address this problem by cutting at their rim first. If you have an auger-type bit of the correct size, with a well-sharpened spur, use that. But if you're going to buy a bit to drill your entrance hole, spend a little extra for a Forstner bit. A spade bit will surely tear the edges of your hole. Take a minute to test the bit you intend to use on a scrap piece of plywood.

For holes over 2", use a hole saw. This is a cup-shaped piece of steel with saw teeth around its rim, attached to a mandrel for mounting in the drill press. Set the drill press for a relatively slow speed. Because it doesn't provide a way for the sawdust to be cleared from its kerf, you'll have to raise the hole saw several times during drilling to clean the gullets between the teeth. Pushing a scrap of wood at a slight angle against the teeth will bump the compacted dust clear. Try to raise the hole saw and clean its teeth before the sawdust starts burning in the kerf. When you've sawn through the workpiece, push the waste disc from the hole saw. The disc comes out easier when it's still warm.

PHOTO 6

DRILLING PILOT HOLES

Either finishing nails or wood screws reinforce most of the joints in these projects. Each fastener requires a pilot hole to make driving it easier and to keep the wood from splitting. Pilot holes for nails need to be smaller in diameter than the nails, of course. Choose a 1/16" bit for 3d and 4d nails, and a 5/62" bit for 6d nails.

Screws present a more complicated situation because they have more parts. A standard, old-fashioned, flat-head wood screw has threads, a root (the solid part inside the threads), a shank, and a conically-shaped head. Ideally, the first part of the pilot bit should drill a hole the size of the root; the next part should be the same diameter and length as the shank; the third part should cut an angled shoulder, or countersink, for the cone under the screw head; and the fourth part should cut a counterbored hole to accommodate the appropriate plug, or "bung." Add to that mess the different lengths of screws in each size, and you see that the problem becomes unmanageable: even if all those sizes of pilot bits were available, you'd go broke buying them. Fortunately, most of us now use drywall screws or decking screws, which are threaded right up to the head, like sheet-metal screws. At least we don't have to allow for the shank any more.

For a screw to help pull the two parts of a joint together, it must slide through the first piece of wood and hold fast in the second piece. In most cases, this happens automatically, because the threaded portion of the screw in the second piece is significantly longer than the threads in the first piece. The threads strip within the first piece so that the head can pull it tight to the second piece. Therefore, the diameter of a proper pilot hole lies somewhere between the root diameter and that of the outside of the threads. The harder the wood, the larger the pilot bit should be.

Several kinds of pilot bits with countersinks and counterbores are available, but most have flaws. The least expensive of these consist of a twisted piece of flat steel. They're not very good at cutting a hole, they dull quickly, and they come in only a few lengths. At the other end of the price scale are tapered bits with adjustable countersinks/counterbores. The bits themselves have a hard time ejecting waste, so they tend to overheat, which dulls their cutting edges. Furthermore, if you look carefully at a screw, you'll see that it's primarily straight-sided, not tapered. But those adjustable countersinks work very well.

And that suggests my preferred solution: a normal twist drill bit with an adjustable countersink/counterbore. (See photo 7.) The countersinks usually have two set screws to hold them onto the bit, and come labeled for particular screw sizes. However, if you use the bit that fits the countersink labeled for your screw, the pilot hole will be too large, because that's the size of the shank (and the threads) of standard wood screws. So use a countersink one size smaller than your screw size, and the twist drill that fits it. For #6 screws, you'd use a #5 countersink with a 1/8" bit. Make sure that the set screws ride in the flutes of the bit, not the flats, and set the countersink just a little short of the length of your screws. Isn't that slick? Just get a #5 and a #7 countersink (don't forget the allen wrench), and you're all set for these projects and most others, as well.

PHOTO 7

PHOTO 8

PHOTO 9

PHOTO 10

SIMPLE GLASS CUTTING

Of course you can have the glass or hardware store cut your glass for you. But they probably charge for each cut, and that could add up quickly, especially in the case of the Octagon House Birdfeeder (see page 89). And what happens if your window holes come out slightly smaller than the drawings show? Back to the hardware store? Why not cut your own glass? I'll tell you how to do it.

Take your list of glass pieces to the store, and buy a standard-size piece of double-strength glass large enough for those pieces and a little more, in case you make a mistake. Purchased this way, glass is cheap. You'll need a glass-cutting tool, too, which you can pick up at the same hardware store. If you already have a glass cutter, take a good look at the cutting wheel. If it shows any rust, you need a new one. In fact, if you're the least bit concerned that it may be dull, buy a new one. You need a good, even score to break double-strength glass accurately.

Work on a flat, smooth surface, such as a piece of plywood. Try to use the glass efficiently as you mark out your pieces with a fine-point marking pen. Avoid trying to break off narrow pieces of glass until you have some experience. Even a fine marking pen makes a wide line if you're measuring sixteenths of an inch, so try making a tiny dot, or use one edge of a line as your mark. When you score the glass, the wheel of the glass cutter must be kept vertical, not tilted, so use the glass cutter to set the position of your straightedge, which will be more than 1⁄16" from your marks. The straightedge itself must be thick enough so that the side of the tool, and not the wheel, rubs against it. Hold at least one end of the straightedge with a spring clamp. To protect your eyes, wear saftey glasses for the next step.

When you're sure of your setup, score the glass in one continuous motion from one edge of the glass to the other, as shown in photo 8. Scoring double-strength glass requires very firm pressure, but you must not go back over the scored line. That will dull your cutting wheel. Make sure you keep the wheel vertical and the side of the tool against your straightedge.

Here comes the exciting part. Remove the spring clamp, and align the scored line with the edge of your work surface. Use the ball end of the glass cutter to tap along the scored line on the side overhanging the edge. The final step requires assured firmness, so make up your mind that this unlikely thing will actually work. Remember that you're holding a piece of liquid that just happens to be extremely viscous. That scored line on top of the glass gives the liquid a chance to separate exactly where you want it to. Hold the glass flat against the work surface with one hand, grasp the overhanging edge with your other hand, closer to the near end of the line, and push down firmly with the base of your thumb. Photo 9 shows the starting position. Keep your arm stiff and push from your shoulder. If you hold the glass correctly, your hand doesn't usually touch the sharp edges of the glass at all. If you're worried about getting cut, wear gloves, or use a folded paper towel to protect your "breaking" hand.

The glass should break cleanly along the scored line. When this works right, you can almost feel the glass ripping. If something else happens, it usually means that your scored line was not continuous or was not strong enough. You can break off small remaining pieces with a pair of pliers, applied gently with its nose to the scored line, but it's often better to start over with a fresh cut.

BIRDHOUSE MATERIALS

PLYWOOD

You've probably noticed that the birdhouses in this book have pretty civilized models—they're not "natural," and they don't pretend to be. Accordingly, we'll be working with pretty civilized materials. The projects specify plywood as the primary building material because it comes in uniform sheets and it doesn't swell or shrink. Solid wood expands and contracts as it gains and loses moisture, and it does so unevenly. Most of the joints in these projects would become loose quickly if they were made from lumber. We'll use solid wood mostly for trim and for pieces that need to be shaped.

When it comes to choosing plywood, you should be concerned with two variables: voids and thickness. Of course, both sides of your plywood should be smooth, without any holes in the surface veneer. Voids are holes in interior layers, that show up as gaps on the edges of the plywood. These must be filled before you paint, both to hide them and to keep water out. So it's best to choose plywood with few voids. Look at the edges of the sheet, and reject plywood that shows many holes. Generally, the more you spend, the fewer voids you should expect. However, you don't need to be so finicky as to buy marine plywood or Baltic birch plywood, both of which have no voids whatsoever. Most of the houses pictured were made with lauan plywood, but you can use material made of any species.

The thickness of a sheet of plywood can vary slightly, and the thicknesses of sheets in the same stack may differ slightly, but these factors do not generally affect the success of a project. More important, plywood manufactured under metric standards is often sold in English measurements, and can be almost 1⁄16" thinner than you're led to believe. The same rule applies to standard plywood, which is generally thinner than its stated size. This won't cause insurmountable problems, but you'll have to adjust any measurements that depend on the thickness of your plywood. For instance, if you're building a box 6" square from ½" plywood that's really 7⁄16" thick, two sides will have to be 5⅛" long. In projects which require stacking multiple thicknesses of plywood, such as the Chrysler Building Nuthatch House (see page 105) or the Tikal I Titmouse House (see below and page 73), you will save yourself trouble by finding full-thickness material. In any case, don't just trust the nominal size—measure it.

THE TIKAL I TITMOUSE HOUSE SHOWN HERE IS MADE ENTIRELY FROM PLYWOOD. YOU CAN CREATE THICK PARTS BY STACKING AND GLUING THINNER PIECES TOGETHER.

SOLID WOOD

You can buy the lumber for these birdhouses at your local lumber yard, home center, or hobby shop. Most of the pieces you'll need are small, so you may be able to use up some of that scrap you've been saving. Remember that hobby shops carry thin pieces of basswood, and even hardwood, for model builders, so use them if you don't own a thickness planer. On the other hand, if your significant other really wants that birdhouse, what better excuse could you find for getting a cute little thicknesser? Just a thought, and I don't even sell tools!

Since you'll probably want to paint your birdhouse, you don't need to worry about rot-resistance in the lumber you use. The woods you're likely to find, pine or cedar, are pretty weather-resistant anyway. The only project that calls for hardwood, the Octagon Birdfeeder (see page below and page 89) does so because lots of tiny bird claws will quickly reduce softwood perches to sawdust. So there again, the species makes less difference than the hardness of the material.

One word about lumber grades: Because the pieces of wood you'll be cutting are small and thin, there's no need to clutter your life with knots. Just buy nice, clear, straight-grained lumber. It's more likely to remain straight after you rip it anyway.

GLUE

Waterproof glues used to be difficult to use (resorcinol) or expensive (epoxy)—or both. Fortunately, within the past few years "Type II" or cross-linking exterior glues have been developed with working properties similar to regular old yellow woodworking glue. While these glues can't claim to be waterproof, they hold up well outdoors, they're reasonably priced, and they don't require mixing. Different brands of exterior woodworking glues have somewhat different consistencies and tackiness, so try a few until you find the brand you like.

THE OCTAGON BIRDFEEDER SHOWN HERE IS CONSTRUCTED PRIMARILY OF PLYWOOD; BUT SOLID HARDWOOD LEDGES, OR PERCHES, AT THE BOTTOM OF THE FEEDER RESIST BIRD CLAWS.

MAKING PATTERNS

Some of the projects in this book include pattern drawings for their curved pieces. In each case, the scale of the drawing is noted. With full-scale drawings, you can either trace the lines you need for your pattern or make a 100 percent photocopy of the figure. (If you have copyright trouble at the copy store, show the clerk this paragraph for reassurance. It's okay, clerk.) With drawings scaled less than full size, you'll have to enlarge the copy appropriately.

However you make your copy, you now have a full-scale drawing on fairly thin paper. If you have only one piece to cut from the pattern, you can stick the drawing directly to the workpiece with spray adhesive or carpet (double-sided) tape. (Read and follow the cautions on the spray can.) Then saw to the outline on the band saw or with a jigsaw, and scrape or peel off the drawing when you're finished.

If you're making a pattern to trace on more than one workpiece, glue the drawing to a sturdier piece of paper—a manilla file folder is perfect, and you probably have one around. Spray adhesive works well for this because it doesn't pucker or change the size of the paper, as water-based glues do. Use a narrow-bladed craft knife or a pair of sharp scissors to cut the tracing lines.

Here are two more things to consider: If the pattern includes a straight line matching the edge of the workpiece, you might leave that line uncut and fold it to automatically align the pattern. If you're working with a half-pattern, you'll have had the foresight to make two copies, of course. Some copy machines will even flip the image for you. Match the centerlines, and tape the halves together before you adhere them to the backing. Matching them with the spray adhesive alone is a one-shot deal—you have approximately a zero chance of getting it right.

ABOUT THE PROJECTS

Many of these birdhouses are modelled on specific buildings designed by well-known architects. I've also included several examples of *vernacular* architecture, houses based on regional forms and materials. Their styles express the combination of several influences, including the tastes of their owners, the skill of their builders, available materials, and technological advances. The history of a vernacular form is often as interesting as the achievement of a particular architect.

The projects are arranged from easiest to most challenging, although the operations you consider difficult will depend on your experience. Read through any project you intend to build, and make sure that you understand the processes involved. Each project lists the materials used to make the birdhouse. If you have not done so already, please read the previous section in Birdhouse Materials about plywood. paying special attention to my warnings about thickness. Next comes a short list of supplies, which includes items you may have to purchase especially for that project. Again, read the instructions to find out how the supplies come into play, and decide what you need.

The cutting list shows all the parts in each project. Its title does not mean that you should start cutting. Successful woodworking involves careful strategy, and sometimes cutting to length is the last, not the first, operation performed on a particular piece. Follow the instructions in order. I have carefully sequenced the steps to help you achieve a good result. Not every step depends on the previous one, it's true, but deviate from their order at your own risk.

SOME RELEVANT TERMINOLOGY

The dimensions listed in the cutting lists and throughout the book show the thickness first, the width second, and the length third. When referring to solid wood, width always means across the grain, while length always indicates the long-grain dimension. If you cut 1" off the end of a 2 x 4, that chunk would measure 1½" x 3½" x 1". In the case of plywood, the dimensions don't relate to grain direction—width is simply shorter than length. Cut your plywood pieces in the most efficient way.

This book uses names for the parts of boards in particular and consistent ways, too. *Face* refers to a wide, long-grain side; *width* is measured across the face. *Edge* refers to a narrow side, where thickness is measured. *End* is the end-grain side of solid wood, and a narrower edge of plywood. *Corners* are where any two or three sides intersect.

OUTDOORS VS. INDOORS

The materials, fasteners, and glue specified in the projects assume that you will mount your birdhouse outdoors. If you do a good job of sealing the birdhouse with filler, primer, and paint, it should withstand weather well, requiring only the sort of maintenance that a wood frame house does. To make your birdhouse last longer, you should always try to employ materials designed for exterior use. If you know that the birdhouse will stay indoors, you can change some of the materials and omit some steps. You can use less-expensive drywall screws instead of decking screws, for instance. All of the birdhouses incorporate ways of opening them for cleaning, so hinges and latches would be unnecessary if the birdhouse is simply a decorative element in your home. You can also leave out the ventilation holes in the projects that call for them.

A WORD ABOUT SAFETY

> ***The only cause of injuries in your shop is you.***

You must be attentive to what you and your tools are doing. Wear ear and eye protection, not just because they reduce eye and ear injuries, but because they reduce distractions. Understand your machinery and the forces it generates. You will notice that some of the photographs in this book show my table saw without its guard in place. This is common practice in all the shops I have visited, a result of the fact that table saw guards prevent several of the operations we often perform. The other guards on my machines stay in place; I value them because they remind me of the dangers involved, not because they protect me from harm. Use guards wherever possible. No guard can keep you from getting hurt, but it can help you stay attentive to the danger. Keep your tools in good working order and keep them sharp. Be particularly wary of machines that seem benign, like the jointer—it can lull you into complacency. If you suspect that a task might be risky on a machine, do it by hand. Hand tools are slower: you make mistakes more slowly and you cut yourself more slowly. Have I made myself clear yet? Okay, just one more.

> ***Machines never make mistakes—only the operator does.***

SALTBOX WREN HOUSE

ARCHITECT: Vernacular

Apparently, saltbox houses were named for their distinctive shape, which is reminiscent of the boxes used to store salt in the seventeenth century. I can't verify the resemblance from personal experience, but it makes as much sense as the other name sometimes applied to these houses—"catslide"—because cats either do or do not like to slide down the long back roofs. Whatever you call it, this is a beautiful and adaptable house form, as the many contemporary saltboxes attest. Build this relatively easy project as a house for wrens or to decorate your own home.

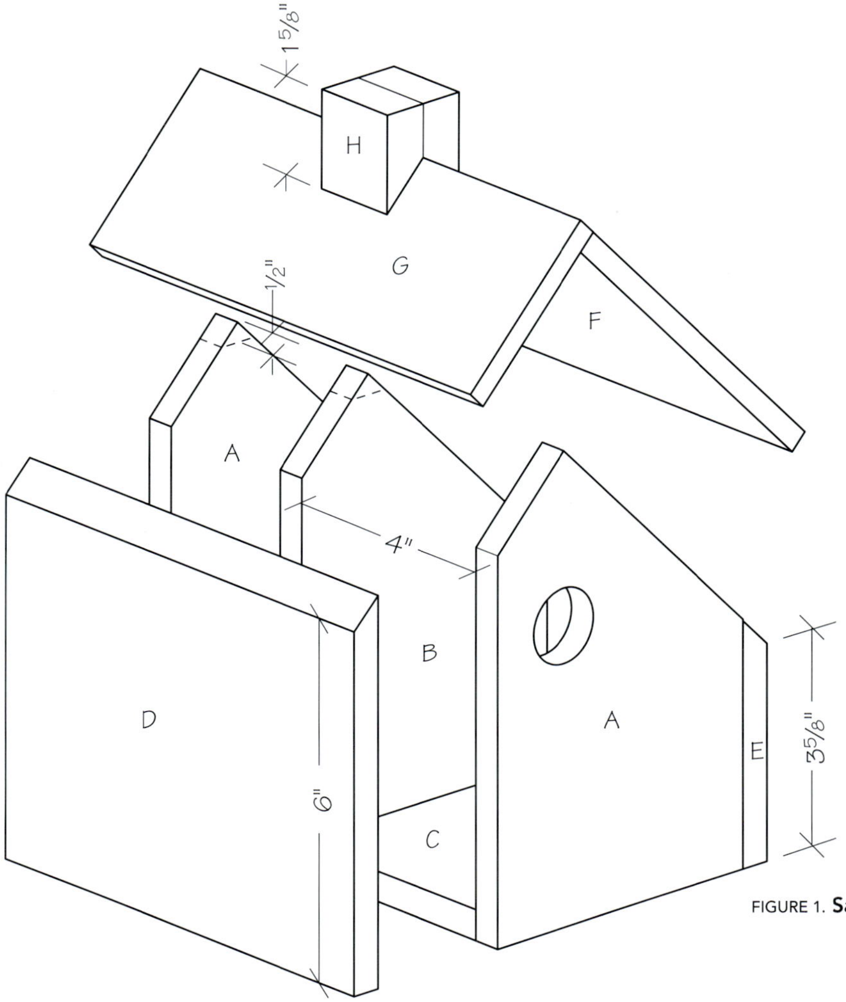

FIGURE 1. **Saltbox Wren House**

CUTTING LIST

CODE	DESCRIPTION	QTY.	MATERIAL	DIMENSIONS
A	Ends	2	plywood	1/2" x 5 1/8" x 7 7/8"
B	Divider	1	plywood	1/2" x 5 1/8" x 7 3/8"
C	Floor	1	plywood	1/2" x 5 1/8" x 7 1/2"
D	Front	1	plywood	1/2" x 6 1/2" x 8 1/2"
E	Back	1	plywood	1/2" x 4 1/8" x 8 1/2"
F	Back roof	1	plywood	3/8" x 6 1/4" x 9"
G	Front roof	1	plywood	3/8" x 3 1/4" x 9"
H	Chimney*	1	1 x 2 pine	1 1/2" x 1 1/2" x 1 5/8"

* Made from two pieces of 1x stock glued together

MATERIALS

1/2" exterior plywood, 1/8 sheet
3/8" exterior plywood, 1/8 sheet
Pine, from scrap

SUPPLIES

3d finishing nails
#6 x 1 1/4" decking screws
1/16" drill bit and 1 1/4" Forstner bit
#6 pilot bit
2 butt hinges, 1" x 1"
1/4 x 2 1/2" eye bolt, washer, and nut (optional)

NOTE: If you plan to use printed house sides, be sure to read Using Printed Decoration on page 139 before you begin to cut any plywood. If your saltbox will never be inhabited by real birds, you may omit the divider (B) and simply nail the floor (C) in place (see step 10).

BUILDING THE WALLS AND FLOOR

1 Start with the ends (A), the divider (B), and the floor (C). Rip a piece of ½" plywood, at least 32" long, to 5⅛" wide. Then cut two 8"-long pieces from it for the ends and one 7½" piece for the floor. The remaining piece will be the divider.

2 Using a combination square and the dimensions in figure 2, mark the roof lines on one of the ends. The roof lines are 45° from the long edges of the end blanks. Transfer the ends of the roof lines to the edges of the plywood, so you'll know where to cut them on the table saw. Stack the two ends together, with their bottom edges aligned and the piece with your layout lines on the bottom. Place the divider on top of the ends, long edges aligned, with its bottom edge ½" in from the bottom edge of the ends. Use a scrap of plywood or the edge of the floor to measure the offset, as shown in photo 1. Hold the stack together with masking tape.

3 Using the line on the edge of the plywood, cut the longer back roof line first. Photo 2 shows this first cut being made with the miter gauge set to 45°. Make the second cut, for the front roof line, square to the first cut. (See photo 3.)

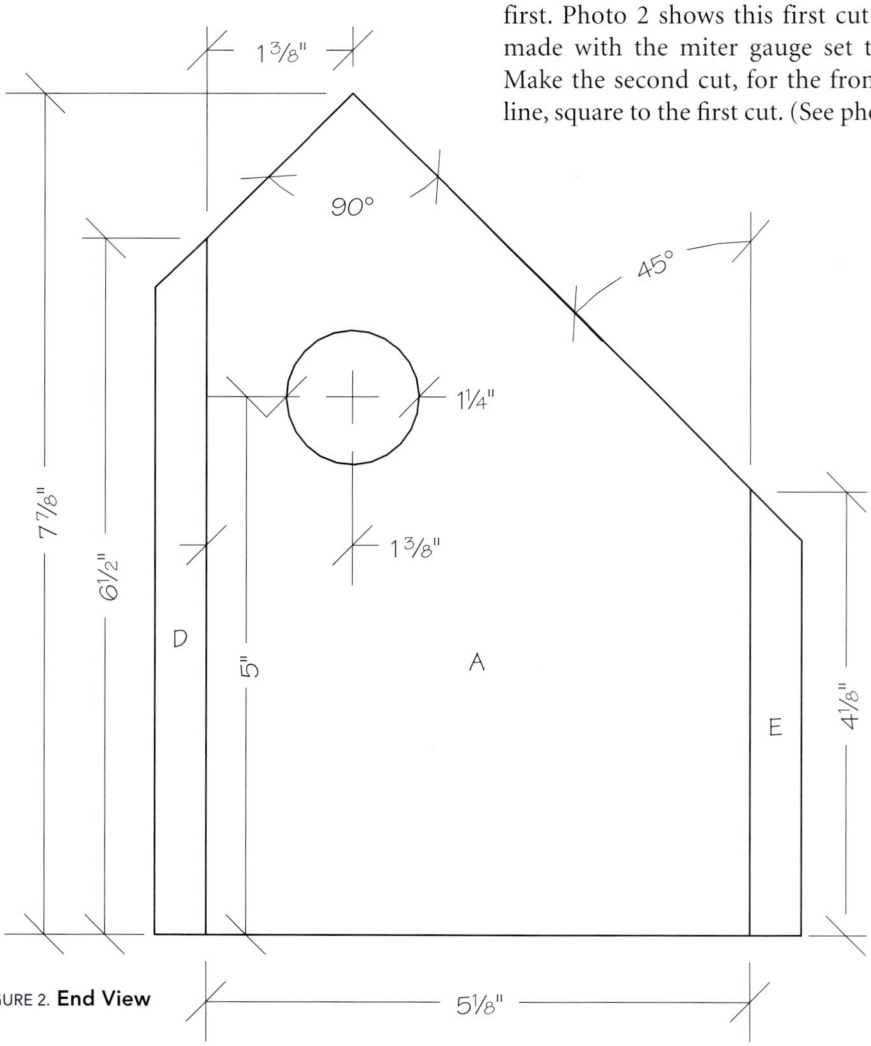

FIGURE 2. **End View**

4 Mark the center of the hole in one of the ends, as shown in figure 2. Use a 1¼" Forstner bit to bore the hole. Remember to back up your work or cut from both sides to prevent tearout.

5 Next, cut the front (D) and back (E). Start by ripping a piece of ½" plywood, about 12" long, to 8½" wide. Cut the front and the back from this piece, mitering their top edges to the dimensions shown in figure 2. Before making the cuts, check your rip fence setting by using the front and back edges of the ends, as shown in photo 4.

6 To prepare for assembling the walls, square a line across the floor, 4" from one end, as shown in figure 1. This marks out the snug nesting area that wrens like. Stand the ends and the front and back in place around the floor, with the nesting area adjacent to the entrance hole. Transfer the line from the floor to the inside faces of the front and the back, and square the lines up the walls.

7 Put all the pieces, including the divider, in place, and then lay the front and back on the bench, as shown in photo 5. Apply glue to the front and back edges of the ends and the divider, and clamp the front and back in place. The outside edges should be flush, and the divider should be even with its pencil lines. When all the walls are clamped in place, remove the floor to make sure it doesn't get glued by mistake.

8 When the glue has dried, drill ¹⁄₁₆" pilot holes, two per joint, at opposing angles, through the front and back and into the ends and the divider. Reinforce the joints with 3d finishing nails, and set the heads.

9 Using a low-angle block plane or your table saw, trim the floor enough to allow it to pivot open on its hinges, which you are about to install.

10 With the house perched on its back roof lines, put the floor in place. Wedge some folded paper or a sliver of wood between the floor and the back to push the floor against the front. Place a butt hinge across the floor/front joint, about 1" from the end of the house, as shown in photo 6. Mark the screw holes, drill ¹⁄₁₆" pilot holes, and drive the screws. Install another hinge at the opposite end of the house.

11 About 1" from the back, drill a #6 pilot hole through the bottom and into the divider. Drive a #6 x 1¼" screw to secure the floor, as shown in photo 6.

PHOTO 4

PHOTO 5

PHOTO 6

SALTBOX ORIGINS

PHOTOS BY THOMAS STENDER

THE ORIGINAL SALTBOXES EVOLVED FROM ENTIRELY practical considerations. When the first English settlers were able to build more substantial houses than the huts they had hurriedly built on arrival in New England, the new houses were still rather small. Nevertheless, they often had two stories, with one room or two rooms per floor. The former had a chimney on one end, serving both floors. When they needed to expand, and could afford to do so, the homeowners added two rooms, one up and one down, on the other side of the chimney. The new four-room house matched those of their neighbors who had built larger homes in the first place.

When they again needed more space, they often added two rooms to the back of the first floor, and extended the back roof line until it was about seven feet from the ground floor, just enough height for a back door. This configuration resulted in the saltbox profile, first seen about 1650. The arrangement proved so practical, especially for those who didn't need or couldn't afford a full, two-story house with four rooms per floor, that saltboxes began to be built whole by about 1675. Their attractive profile must have encouraged the building of these non-incremental saltboxes.

For all their practicality in solving the problems of adding on, saltboxes have some inherent disadvantages. The expanse of back roof disallows windows on that side of the second-floor rooms. That fact, combined with the low first-floor ceiling heights of early saltboxes, make them quite dark. In addition, the spaces under the roof tend to be less usable than normal attics. For these reasons, new saltboxes often have open plans, cathedral ceilings, and dormers or skylights interrupting the back roof.

FIGURE 3.
Chimney Blank

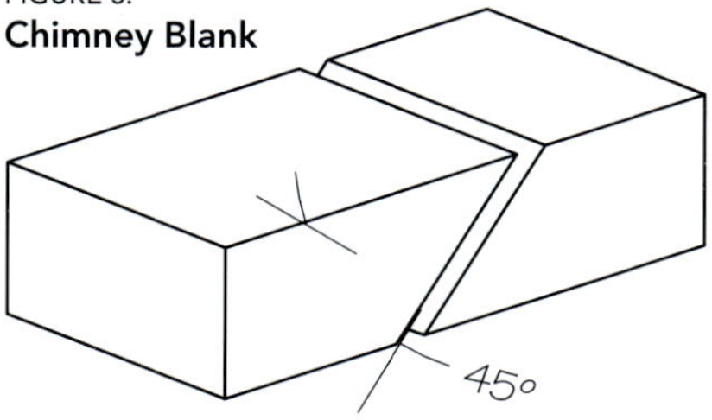

ADDING THE ROOF AND CHIMNEY

1 Cut the back roof (F) and the front roof (G) to size. Apply glue to the top edge of the back roof, and clamp the roof pieces together, with their ends even and the joint flush on the outside (see photo 7). You can use the house as a clamping jig to make sure that the roofs are square to each other and that they fit the ends.

2 When the glue has dried, drill pilot holes, and reinforce the roof joint with 3d finishing nails. Set the nail heads.

3 To make the chimney (H), begin by cutting a piece of 1 x 2 pine 4" long. Then crosscut a 45° miter at the center of the blank, as shown in figure 3. Glue and clamp the two halves together, forming a vee that will fit the peak of the roof. When the glue has cured, crosscut the chimney 1⅝" long.

4 Hold the chimney in place, centered on the roof peak, while you trace its outline on the roof. Don't install the chimney yet.

5 If you are going to hang your saltbox outdoors, drill a ¼" hole down through the center of the chimney and through the roof pieces for a 2½"-long eye bolt.

PHOTO 7

FINISHING THE SALTBOX

1 Painting the house is much easier before you install the roof and chimney, but you should avoid painting the areas of the roof where it will be glued to the house sides. Place the roof assembly on top of the house, centered lengthwise, and trace the top edges of the walls onto the bottoms of the roof pieces. Don't paint inside those lines! And don't paint the top edges of the house, either. Leave a bare place for glue where the chimney goes on the roof, too. So much to remember!

2 Fill all the nail holes, and sand the house, roof, and chimney. Prime all the surfaces to be painted, then sand them again.

3 Refer to Finishing your Birdhouse on page 138 for painting ideas and for information on using printed house sides.

4 Once your finish has dried, apply glue to the top edges of the walls and the divider. Center the roof assembly over the house sides and hold it in place while you drill 1⁄16" pilot holes through the roof and into the edges of the ends, two near each end of the front roof and three near each end of the back roof. Drill these holes square to the roof surface, not vertically, so that they will help support the weight of the house. Drive 3d nails and set their heads. Fill these holes carefully, and touch up the roof paint.

5 Glue the chimney to the roof, holding it firmly in place until the glue begins to set.

DUTCH GABLED CHICKADEE HOUSE

ARCHITECT: Vernacular

Gabled buildings in the Low Countries and northern Germany tended toward the ornate. I guess that's why they call it baroque, isn't it? I've simplified the decoration on this house as much as possible, so feel free to embellish it as much as you want. I don't think your chickadees will mind. Build this relatively simple project and give them a pretty home close to yours.

FIGURE 1.
Dutch Gabled Chickadee House

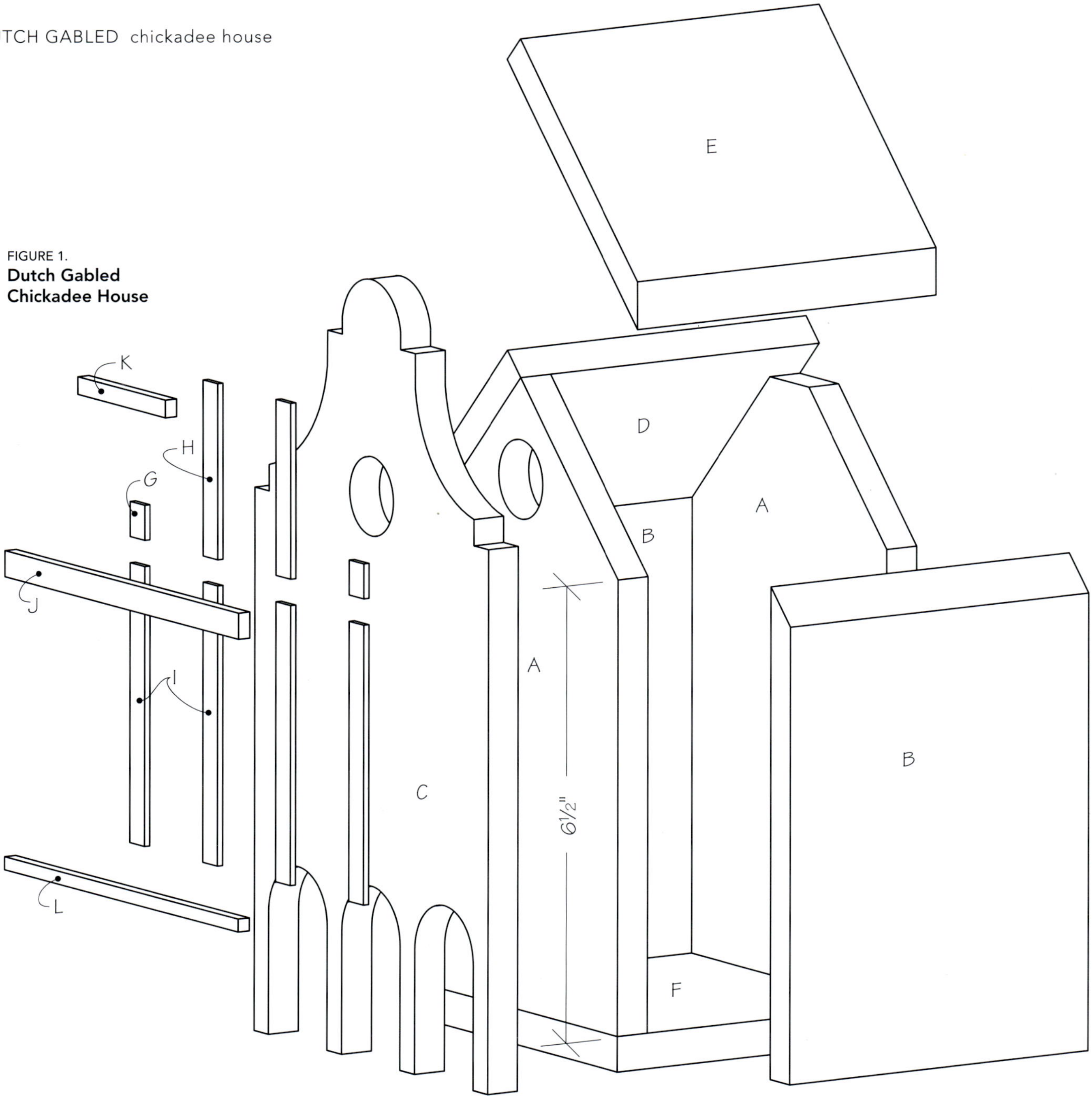

CUTTING LIST

CODE	DESCRIPTION	QTY.	MATERIAL	DIMENSIONS
A	Ends	2	plywood	½" x 5" x 9"
B	Sides	2	plywood	½" x 5" x 7"
C	Gabled front	1	plywood	½" x 6" x 11¼"
D	Left roof	1	plywood	½" x 4¼" x 5"
E	Right roof	1	plywood	½" x 4¾" x 5"
F	Floor	1	plywood	½" x 5" x 5"
G	Short vertical trim	2	basswood	3/32" x ⅜" x ½"
H	Medium vertical trim	2	basswood	3/32" x ⅜" x 2½"
I	Long vertical trim	4	basswood	3/32" x ⅜" x 4"
J	Middle trim	1	basswood	3/16" x ⅜" x 6"
K	Top trim	1	basswood	3/16" x ¼" x 2¼"
L	Lower trim	1	basswood	3/16" x 3/16" x 6"

MATERIALS

½" exterior plywood, ⅛ sheet

3/32" basswood or balsa, 1" x 12"

3/16" basswood or balsa, 1" x 6"

SUPPLIES

3d finishing nails

#6 x 1¼" decking screws

1/16" drill bit and 1⅛" Forstner bit

#6 pilot bit

NOTE: If you want your chickadees to be happy and cool, remember to cut ½" from the top of the back end (A) for ventilation.

CUTTING AND ASSEMBLING THE HOUSE

1 Cut the two ends (A) to size. Use a miter square or a combination square to draw the 45° roof lines. Photo 1 shows the roof lines being sawn using a miter gauge with a stop to make sure that the sides are even.

2 Cut two sides (B) to size, again using the miter gauge. Note that their top edges are bevelled 45° to match the roof lines. In photo 2, the stop on the miter gauge ensures that the sides will be the same height.

3 The width of the gabled front (C) must equal the width of one end plus two side thicknesses. Don't assume that your plywood is exactly ½" thick—stack those pieces together and measure the sandwich. Then cut the front to that width and at least 11 1/16" long. You'll cut it to final length later when you cut the scrollwork at the top of the gable.

PHOTO 1

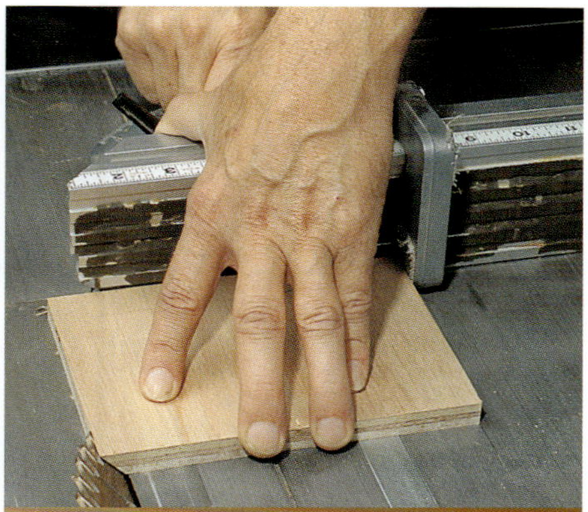

PHOTO 2

PHOTO 3

PHOTO 4

4 Place one end flat against the front, with ½" (or a plywood thickness) of the front protruding on each side and on the bottom, as shown in photo 3. Clamp those pieces together, and turn them over so that you're working on the front. Mark the center of the entrance hole as specified in figure 2. Bore a 1⅛" hole at that point.

5 Apply glue to the vertical edges of the ends, and clamp the sides to the ends, so that the bevelled top edges of the sides are flush with the angled ends. Make sure that the outside surfaces are flush. Drill three angled 1/16" pilot holes through each joint, as shown in photo 4. Drive 3d finishing nails into the pilot holes and set the heads.

6 Cut a piece of plywood 5" wide and about 10" long for the two roof pieces. Using the rip fence this time, as shown in photo 5, with the table-saw blade tilted to 45°, cut the left roof (D) a little oversize. Put the left roof in place to gauge how much to trim, move the rip fence, and cut the left roof again so that its square edge meets the roof peak and its bevelled edge is flush with the house side.

7 With the left roof held in place, drill 1⁄16" pilot holes through it into the top edges of the ends. Apply glue to those edges and to the top edge of the left side. Nail the left roof in place, being very careful to keep the edges flush with the ends and sides of the house.

8 Cut the right roof (E) in the same way as you cut the left roof, aligning its top (square) edge with the face of the left roof. Drill pilot holes, glue, and nail it in place as before. Make sure you've set all the nail heads. You can go ahead and fill them all now, since you're finished nailing.

9 The floor (F) will be attached to the ends with screws to facillitate cleaning the birdhouse each season, so cut it for a sliding fit between the sides. The ends of the floor should be flush with the outsides of the ends.

10 With the floor held in place, drill pilot holes for #6 screws through the floor and into the bottom edges of the ends, two per end. Drive 1¼" screws to secure the floor.

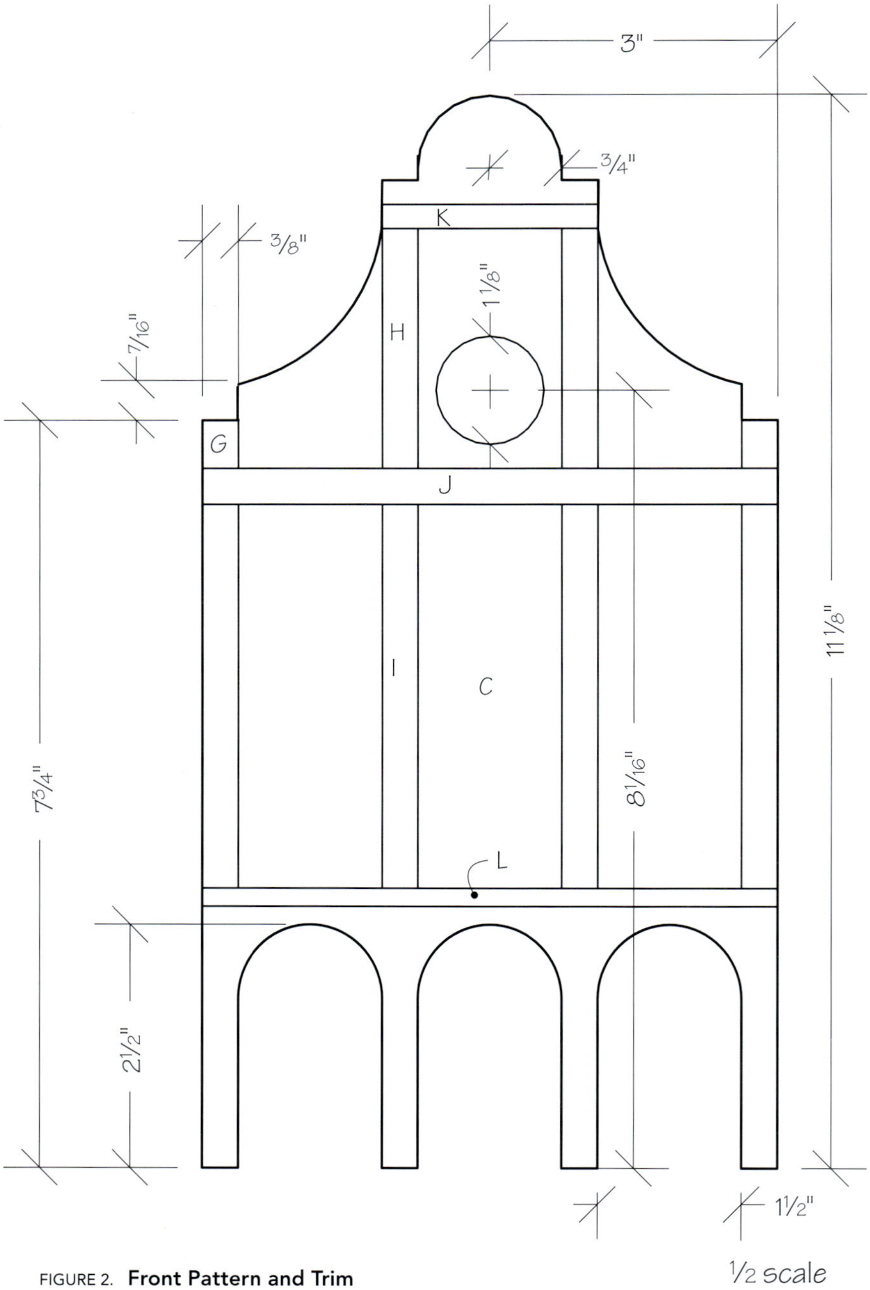

FIGURE 2. **Front Pattern and Trim**

SECULAR GOTHIC

FROM THE BEGINNING, ARCHITECTURE HAS EXPRESSED ITSELF most forcefully in sacred buildings—although recently part of that role has been usurped by museums—temples, cathedrals, churches, and now, temples of culture. Important religious buildings display the architectural style of their time, and they have survived because they continue to fulfill their function. Fewer secular public buildings of significance remain, such as the Coliseum in Rome. Only in the eighteenth century did they begin to carry their architectural weight, in palaces and governmental buildings in Europe and, somewhat later, in the United States. We tend to think of the history of important private or corporate buildings as beginning in the nineteenth century, spurred especially by Chicago architects, such as Louis Sullivan, designer of the Carson Pirie Scott department store. And significant domestic architecture has a spotty story, especially if we omit the houses of aristocrats, which we may consider quasi-governmental.

In northern Europe and the Low Countries, however, the Gothic and Baroque styles were adopted by the most powerful business interests of the day and by prosperous burghers as well. Urban centers in that region retained the densely packed, narrow building lots of the medieval towns from which they grew. As trade revived, the trade and commercial guilds became prosperous and began building headquarters around the central plazas. Constricted by their sites, these buildings had only their facades with which to express the importance, as well as the function, of their owners. While their roofs are steeply peaked, presumably to protect against a wet climate, one would hardly notice them from the street, so imposing are their false fronts.

Elements of the Gothic and Baroque, progressively more decorative, found places in low relief on the gables. Both round and pointed arches framed their arcades, while elaborate steps and robust ogee curves shaped their top profiles. The guilds often topped their facades with a symbol of their trade. We refer to these buildings as gabled because their fronts elaborate their gable ends. The rectangle topped by a triangle simply became unable to contain the exuberance and pride of an emerging middle class.

PHOTO BY MICHAEL BUSSELLE. ©CORBIS IMAGES

CUTTING THE GABLED FRONT AND PAINTING THE HOUSE

1 Make a half-pattern for the top shape of the gabled front, using figure 2 as a guide. Also, make a pattern for one of the arches. See Making Patterns on page 14 for some useful tips. Another option, if you prefer to forgo pattern-making, is to lay out the parts with a tape measure, and use a compass to draw the curves.

2 Trace the pattern for the top shape onto the front, with the uppermost point 11⅛" from the bottom. Trace three arches along the bottom of the front. Adjust the width of the arch pattern so that you leave four ⅜"-wide posts.

3 Cut the top shape and the arches on the band saw or with a jigsaw. Be careful to avoid breaking the posts. Sand the edges of the front thoroughly, while maintaining their shapes. Hold 100-grit sandpaper around suitable flat and rounded pieces of wood, and sand straight across the edges. Keep the curves fair and the straight lines straight. Sand again with 150-grit sandpaper. Sand the house, too, while you're at it.

4 Cut all the trim pieces (G–L) to size, making sure that the lengths of the middle and lower trim (J and L) match the width of the gabled front. Sand, prime, and paint all visible surfaces of the trim.

5 If you intend to paint the space "behind" the arches a different color than the edges of the arches, trace the front arches onto the end with the entrance hole. Then prime and paint inside the traced areas and the arch edges, leaving enough bare wood for gluing the posts to the house end. You may wish to mix a slightly darker color for the edges of the arches, and a darker one still for the spaces under the arches.

6 Lay out the trim pieces on the front, aligning the vertical trim (G, H, and I) with the posts between the arches. Trace all of the trim onto the front. Remove the trim, then prime and paint the front, leaving some bare wood for gluing the trim in place.

7 Glue and clamp the short vertical trim (G) first. Spring clamps work well for this job. You may need plywood clamping pads to spread pressure evenly over the longer trim pieces.

8 If you have more clamps, or as soon as the glue sets, glue the middle trim in place, butted against the bottom of the short vertical trim. Then work upward and downward from the middle trim to apply the rest of the trim pieces.

9 Remove the floor, and then glue the front to the end with the entrance hole. Use plenty of clamps to hold everything in place until the glue cures.

10 Prime and paint the rest of the house.

CAPE COD
BLUEBIRD HOUSE

ARCHITECT: Vernacular

Cape Cod houses are so plentiful in America that there's a reasonable chance you're sitting in one right now. This bluebird house provides a good beginner's project, especially if you omit the dormers. You can also use it as a starting point to design your own houses for other species of birds. Consult the chart on page 136 for their preferred dimensions. Alternatively, you can make a smaller, purely decorative version for your home—maybe even a copy of your own house!

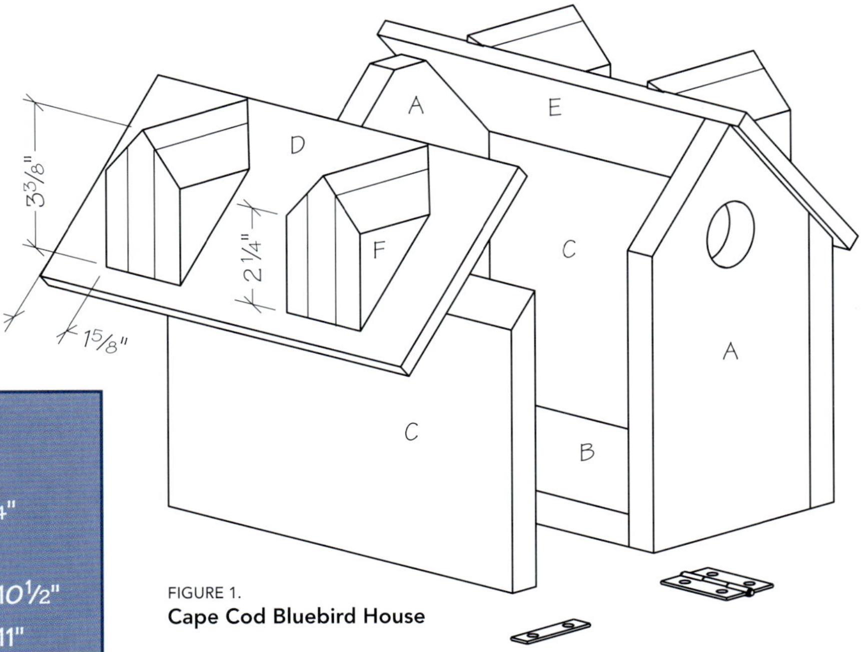

FIGURE 1.
Cape Cod Bluebird House

CUTTING LIST

CODE	DESCRIPTION	QTY.	MATERIAL	DIMENSIONS
A	Ends	2	plywood	3/4" x 5" x 9 1/4"
B	Floor	1	plywood	3/4" x 5" x 9"
C	Sides	2	plywood	3/4" x 6 3/4" x 10 1/2"
D	Front roof	1	plywood	3/8" x 5 3/8" x 11"
E	Back roof	1	plywood	3/8" x 5" x 11"
F	Dormers*	4	pine	2 1/4" x 3 3/8" x 3 3/8"

* Made from three pieces of 1x stock glued together

NOTE: If you plan to use printed decoration to finish your house, as described on page 139, you'll want to delay adding the dormers to the roof and the roof to the house. Even if you'll be painting your house, consider painting these pieces before assembling them.

MATERIALS

3/8" exterior plywood, 1/8 sheet

3/4" exterior plywood, 1/8 sheet

Pine, 1 x 3 x 5'

SUPPLIES

3d finishing nails

4d finishing nails

#6 x 1 5/8" decking screws

1/16" drill bit and 1 1/2" Forstner bit

#6 pilot bit

2 butt hinges, 1 1/2" x 1 1/2"

2 mending plates, 2"

PHOTO 1

PHOTO 2

PHOTO 3

ASSEMBLING THE HOUSE WALLS

1 Begin by cutting the ends (A) to size, following the dimensions in figure 2. The roof lines form 45° angles with the edges of the boards. Mark their positions and cut them on the table saw. Set the miter gauge to 45°, and use a stop to make all four cuts at an equal distance from the bottoms of the ends, as shown in photo 1.

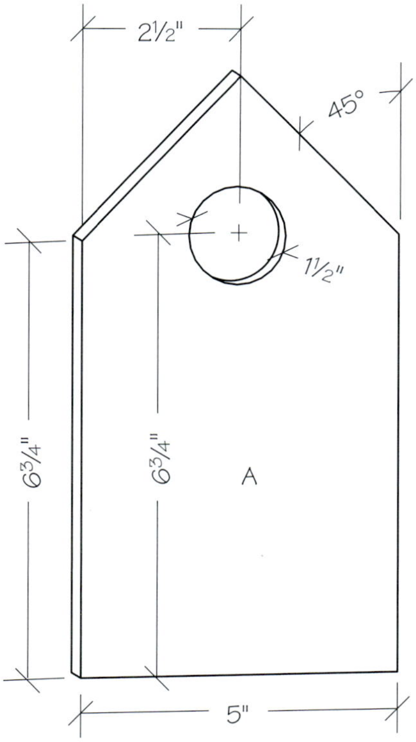

FIGURE 2. **Entrance End**

2 Mark a center for the entrance hole on one of the ends, as shown in figure 2. Bore a 1½" hole at that point (see photo 2). Use your table saw to cut ½" from the top of the other end to provide ventilation.

3 Cut the floor (B) to size.

4 Cut two sides (C) to length, each slightly longer than the length of the floor plus two end thicknesses. This allows a little clearance for the hinged floor.

5 Cut a 45° bevel on the top edge of each side, so that the wider face matches the sides of the ends. Refer to figure 1. You may want to leave a little extra to plane off after you attach the sides to the ends.

6 Apply glue to the edges of the sides, and clamp the sides to the ends, with their outside and bottom edges flush. Drill $\frac{1}{16}$" pilot holes through the sides and well into the ends. Two holes per joint, drilled at opposing angles, as shown in photo 3, will do the trick. Drive 4d finishing nails into the pilot holes, setting their heads.

7 Install a pair of butt hinges along the bottom of one side, about 1½" from each end, as shown in photo 4. The pin of the hinge should be centered on the edge.

8 Slide the floor into place, and screw the loose hinge leaves to it. If the floor is too wide, as is likely, plane a slight bevel on its free edge to allow it to rotate into position.

9 Install two mending plates on the bottom edge of the side, opposite the hinges, and onto the floor to hold it in place (see photo 4). To clean out the nesting box, you'll unscrew the plates and swing the floor down on its hinges.

PHOTO 4

PHOTO 5

PHOTO 6

PHOTO 7

PHOTO 8

MAKING THE ROOF AND ADDING THE DORMERS

1 Cut the front roof (D) and the back roof (E) to size on the table saw.

2 Apply glue to a long edge of the narrower back roof, and clamp the front roof to that edge. Use the house as a gluing jig to make sure that the roofs meet at a right angle. Are the ends even, and is the joint flush on the outside? Good. Then reinforce the roof joint with 3d finishing nails driven at opposing angles through 1⁄16" pilot holes.

3 We'll make the dormers (F) from three thicknesses of pine glued together. Prepare three pieces of 3⁄4"-thick pine, each at least 3½" wide and 18" long. Apply glue to the joining surfaces, and clamp the stack together with its long edges aligned. Use enough glue and plenty of clamps. You should see a little glue squeezing out all along the joints. Photo 5 shows a good way to align the stack. Clamp scrap pieces of plywood to the edges of the stack before applying pressure to the gluing clamps. Just remember to remove the scraps before the glue begins to set.

4 When the glue has dried, joint or rip one edge of the stack straight and square to its faces.

5 Crank the table-saw blade over to 45°, and set the rip fence 2¼" from the open side of the blade, measured at the table (see photo 6). With the jointed edge against the rip fence, rip the stack once with each of its faces down. The second of these cuts is shown in photo 7.

6 Reset the blade to 90°, and use the miter gauge to trim the ends of the blank square. Then crosscut the blank in half. You'll save yourself some setup time later if you use a stop on your miter gauge to cut two pieces of equal length.

(You can cut the dormers from these two blanks safely if you follow my directions in the next three steps. If you choose another method, make sure that you work safely, with your fingers out of harm's way. If you don't have a table saw, you can cut the miters with a handsaw or on the band saw, then clean up the sawn faces with a low-angle block plane or rough sandpaper laid flat on your bench.)

7 You're ready to cut the bottoms of the individual dormers. We'll cut the largest dormers that we can from the blanks. Set the miter gauge to 45°, with the end nearer the blade ahead. Hold one of the stack pieces with its peak against the miter gauge and the leading corner just at the opposite side of the saw blade. Set your stop against the trailing end of the workpiece to help hold everything in place. This setup is shown in photo 8.

Have a waste stick ready to shoo the cutoff dormer away from the blade *and toward you!* When you're sure that everything is ready, make that miter cut, holding the workpiece firmly and feeding steadily. Then make the same cut on the second blank. Aren't you glad you cut both of them the same length?

PHOTO BY THOMAS STENDER

THE ESSENTIAL HOUSE

THE OLDEST KNOWN CAPE COD HOUSE isn't even on Cape Cod, it's in Connecticut. That makes some sense, because the Cape Cod is the most ubiquitous house form in America. Although Capes are easy to identify, they're hard to define. They originated as developments of the huts that seventeenth-century colonists knew in England, and that are still occupied in the west of Ireland, for example. Such houses had one main room with a heavy fireplace at one end. Their steep roofs allowed for a sleeping loft, and the main door entered a roof wall, not a gable end.

The Cape Cod house, as we have come to know it, has an uninterrupted roof line parallel with the front of the house, and is of wood frame construction. The roof pitches steeply enough to provide living space beneath it. We define half, three-quarter, and full Capes as those having two windows on one side of the door, three windows divided by the door, and four windows with a central door, respectively. As the size of Capes grew, two to five dormers were commonly added to augment the light from windows in the gable ends, enabling second stories to be partitioned. Even early Capes were sizeable—34 to 40 feet long and 28 feet deep.

As a simple and easily built house type, the Cape Cod remained popular well into the twentieth century, but its numbers surged after World War II. In 1947, William and Alfred Levitt began building inexpensive houses on Long Island, New York, in a development they humbly called Levittown. These "Cape Coddages" were erected on 25- x 32-foot concrete slabs about 100 feet apart, and were finished by a series of specialized subcontractor crews. The Levitts kept their house prices low by owning most of their suppliers of raw materials and by standardizing component parts. For $7,990, buyers got a two-bedroom house with a living room, bathroom, unfinished attic; and a kitchen outfitted with sinks, a refrigerator/freezer, a two-oven stove, and a Bendix washing machine. Using a sort of inverse assembly-line procedure, the Levitts built 17,442 houses between 1947 and 1951—or one house for every 15 minutes of working time. The facades of the Cape Coddages changed from year to year, and at least five variations were offered each year, but the basic form remained that of the adaptable Cape.

PHOTO 9

PHOTO 10

PHOTO 11

8 Use one of the cut dormers to help cut the third and fourth dormers. Put the square end of one of the dormers against the stop, with its peak against the miter gauge. Then place the angled end of one of the stacked pieces against the angled end of the dormer. Move the stop (and the two pieces of wood) closer to the blade to cut another dormer from the blank. In photo 9, I've separated the parts slightly to show their relative positions. When everything is set, think pure thoughts while you cut the third dormer. Finally, cut the fourth dormer from the remaining blank. Whew! The nasty stuff is over.

9 With the front roof flat on your bench, arrange two of the dormers on the roof, each 1⅝" from an end of the roof, as shown in figure 1. The top points of the dormers should just touch the peak edge of the roof. Use a pencil to trace the outlines of the dormers onto the roof. Put a dollop of glue (that's more than a drop and less than a puddle) on the back of each dormer, and reposition it on the roof. Push each dormer down firmly (see photo 10); there's no need for clamps (as if you could clamp them). When the glue begins to set, glue the dormers to the back roof in the same way.

10 When the glue has cured, drill two pilot holes through the roof and into each dormer. Hold the dormer while drilling and while driving the screws to avoid breaking the glue joint (see photo 11).

11 Set the roof assembly on top of the house walls, centering it lengthwise. Drill 1⁄16" pilot holes through the roof and into the ends (A). Eight holes should be plenty. Drive 3d nails into the pilot holes and set their heads.

PAINTING THE HOUSE

1 Fill all nail holes with putty. Then sand the house thoroughly and paint it with a good-quality exterior primer.

2 Sand the primer coat before proceeding with the finish coats. You'll find helpful finishing tips on page 138.

CARPENTER GOTHIC

TREE SWALLOW HOUSE

ARCHITECT: Vernacular

We might think of Carpenter Gothic as a small-town or rural variant of Victorian style—a way to achieve "fancy" without getting too involved with theoretical notions of taste or consistency. Many of these "Gingerbread Houses" make up in exuberance what they lack in formal references. There's a practical limit to how much fancy one can pack into a house less than a foot tall, and I've chosen the middle ground, based on a house in my neighborhood. Feel free to add any gimcracks and geegaws that appeal to you. Just remember: In the public arena, propriety is all. You gotta love those wacky Victorians.

MATERIALS

3/4" exterior plywood, 1/4 sheet

3/8" exterior plywood, 1 square foot

Pine, from scrap

SUPPLIES

3d finishing nails

4d finishing nails

6d finishing nails

#6 x 1 5/8" decking screws

1/16" and 5/64" drill bits, 1 1/2" Forstner bit

#6 pilot bit

2 butt hinges, 1" x 1"

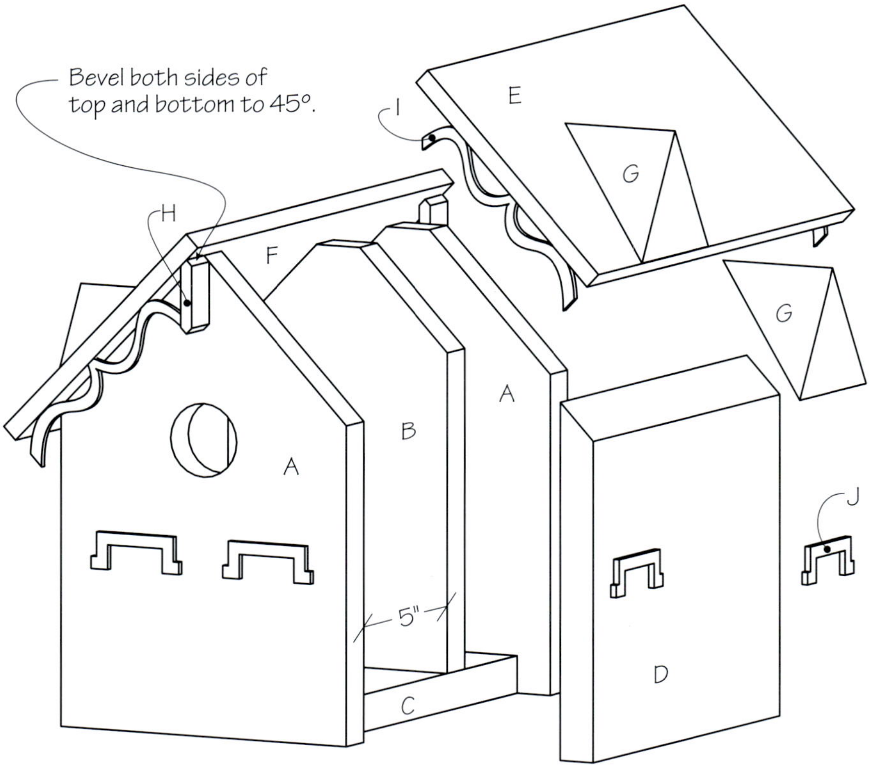

FIGURE 1. **Carpenter Gothic Tree Swallow House**

BUILDING THE HOUSE

1 Cut out the ends (A), divider (B), and floor (C), following the dimensions in the cutting list and in figure 2. Cut ½" from the peaks of the back end and the divider, as shown in figure 1, to provide ventilation for the swallow family.

2 Mark the center of the entrance hole on the front end, using the information in figure 2, and bore a 1½" hole.

3 Cut out the sides (D), bevelling their top edges at 45°, tilting the saw blade and using the rip fence on your table saw.

4 Square a line across the floor, 5" from its front end, as shown in figure 1. Position the divider just behind that line, clamp the pieces together, and drill two #6 pilot holes, well countersunk, through the floor and into the bottom of the divider. Secure the floor with 1⅝" screws, but do not glue this joint, so that the floor can be removed for housecleaning.

CUTTING LIST

CODE	DESCRIPTION	QTY.	MATERIAL	DIMENSIONS
A	Ends	2	plywood	3/4" x 6 1/2" x 9 3/4"
B	Divider	1	plywood	3/4" x 5" x 9"
C	Floor	1	plywood	3/4" x 5" x 8"
D	Sides	2	plywood	3/4" x 7 1/4" x 8"
E	Right roof	1	plywood	3/8" x 5 1/2" x 11"
F	Left roof	1	plywood	3/8" x 5 7/8" x 11"
G	Dormers*	4	plywood	3" x 2 1/2" x 2 1/2"
H	Peak posts	2	pine	1/4" x 3/4" x 1 1/2"
I	Scrolls	4	pine	1/8" x 1" x 5 1/2"
J	Window trim	8	pine	1/8" x 3/4" x 2"

* Made from plywood pieces glued together

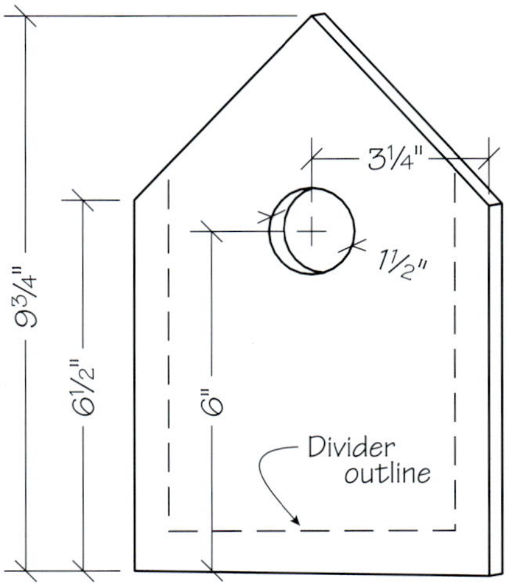

FIGURE 2. **End**

PHOTO 1

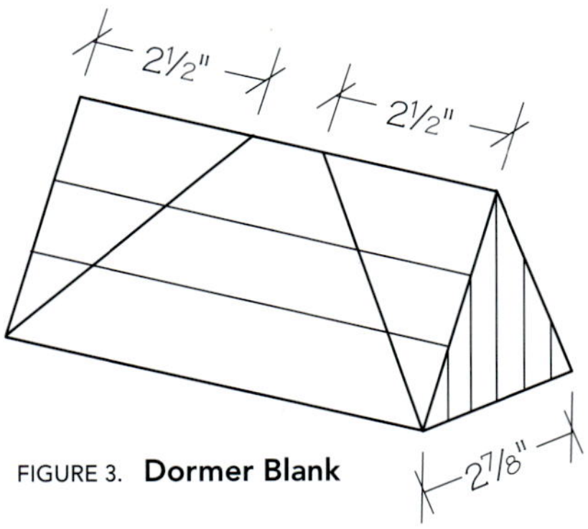

FIGURE 3. **Dormer Blank**

PHOTO 2

5 Square a line vertically up the inside face of each side, 5" from its front end. Glue only the vertical edges of the divider, and align the divider with the lines on the sides while you clamp the sides in place. The bottom edges of the sides should be flush with the bottom of the floor. Drill angled 5/64" pilot holes, and drive 6d finishing nails to fasten the sides to the divider, as shown in photo 1.

6 Fasten the ends to the sides in the same way, gluing only the edges of the sides.

7 Reduce the size of the floor enough so that it will rotate on hinges fastened to the bottom edge of the front end, using a hand plane or some coarse sandpaper. Then screw two hinges in place, as shown in photo 2. Position the hinges about 1 1/4" from the outsides of the house.

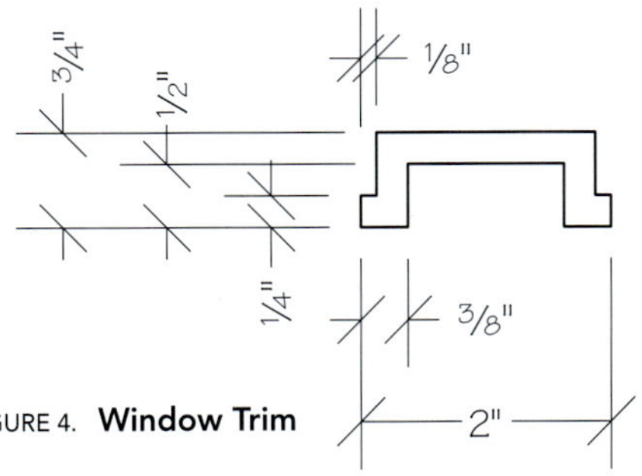

FIGURE 4. **Window Trim**

ADDING THE DORMERS AND ROOF

1 Cut the roofs (E and F).

2 Begin the dormers (G) by gluing plywood pieces into a 2½" x 3" x 12" stack. When the glue has dried, draw a line down the center of a 3" face. Trim the ends of the stack, and cut it in half lengthwise, producing two pieces about 6" long.

3 Set your band-saw table to 30°, and saw just outside the centerlines to form two triangular prisms, as shown in photos 3 and 4. Save the cutoff pieces.

4 Plane or sand the two sawn faces of each prism to smooth them and to make the peak sharp and straight.

5 Draw two diagonal lines on a sawn face of each prism, as shown in figure 3. Tape a cutoff to the other sawn face to support the prism, and, with the table returned to 0°, saw to the diagonal lines, as shown in photo 5.

PHOTO 3

PHOTO 4

PHOTO 5

PHOTO 6

6 Sand the bottom of each dormer to remove the band-saw marks. Test it for flatness against the face of a roof.

7 Follow the dimensions in figure 5 to position the dormers at the bottom edges of the roofs, and mark their places. Apply glue to the bottom of each dormer, and hold it in place until the glue begins to set.

8 When the glue has dried, clamp each roof in a vise, and hold each dormer in place while you drill a #6 pilot hole through the roof and into the dormer (see photo 6). Then fasten the dormers with 1⅝" screws. Before you add the roofs to the house, remove the floor, in case it needs some persuasion from the top.

9 Apply glue to the top edges of the ends and sides, and fasten the roofs—narrower right roof first—with 3d finish nails driven into angled 1/16" pilot holes. Before adding the left roof, spread some glue along the top edge of the right roof. Finally, secure the roof peak with nails.

10 Before going on to trim the house, set all nail heads and putty the holes.

ADDING THE TRIM

1 The trim pieces are delicate, but they "make" the Carpenter Gothic look. To avoid breaking them, be sure to support the stock well while you're sawing and sanding. Cut out the peak posts (H), as shown in figure 1. It's faster and safer to cut these small pieces with a fine-toothed handsaw, such as a dozuki, than to risk cutting them with power tools. You can simply cut them to length, and then shave the mitered ends with a low-angle block plane, as shown in photo 7. Glue them against the ends under the roof at the peak by holding them in place until the glue grabs.

2 Prepare stock for the scrolls (I) and window trim (J), but make the eight pieces for the window trim at least 5" long.

3 Tape the eight pieces of window-trim stock together in a stack. Refer to figure 4 to lay out the shape near one end of the stack. Use a dado blade or a regular crosscut blade on your table saw to cut the notches, beginning at the end of the stock and working across, as shown in photo 8. Hold a scrap piece of pine behind the stack to limit tearout and to keep those small pieces from breaking. When you've established the shape, cut the trim to length, with the final cut freeing the trim from the stack.

FIGURE 5. **Dormer and Window Trim Positions**

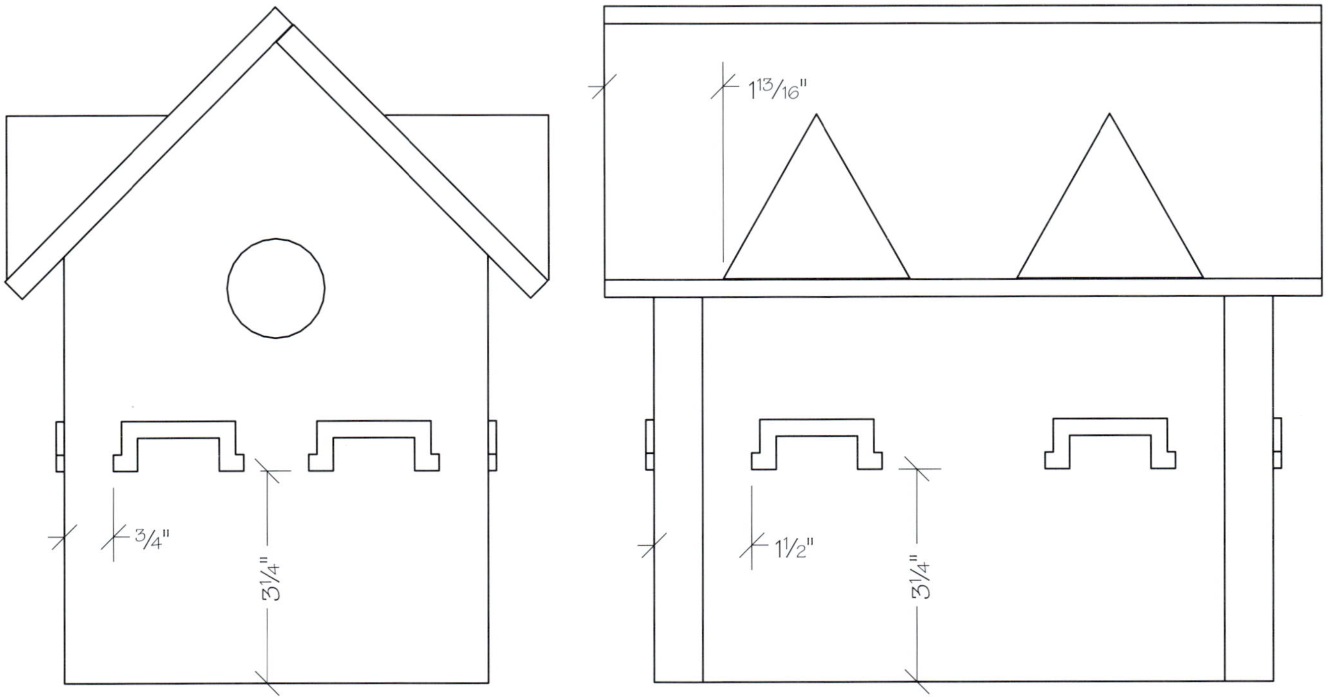

4 Use the information in figure 5 to position the trim on the house. Glue each piece of trim in place, holding it firmly until the glue begins to set.

5 Cut a 45° angle on one end of each scroll blank. Make a pattern for the scrolls from figure 6. (For more information, see Making Patterns on page 14.) Stack the scroll blanks and trace the pattern on the top one. Tape the blanks together at one end. You'll have to move the tape partway through the sawing process.

6 Use a narrow blade on the band saw or a scrollsaw to shape the scrolls, as shown in photo 9. Sand the sawn edges carefully. You'll glue the scrolls to the roof at three places and to the peak post in one place, so don't saw or sand those areas.

7 Put a drop of glue on each contact point of a scroll, and hold it in place at the edge of the roof until the glue cures enough to hold it. Glue on the other three scrolls in the same way.

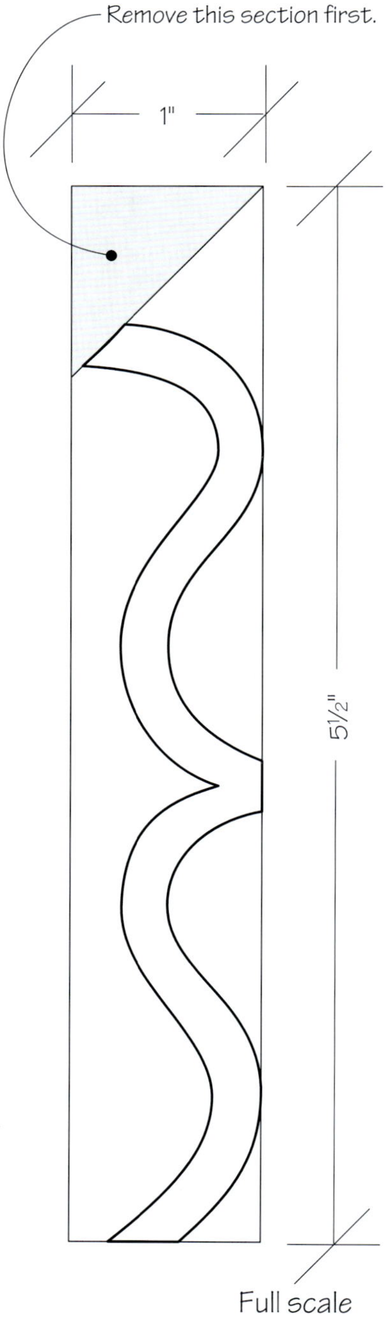

FIGURE 6. **Scroll Pattern**

HOUSEPAINTING

1 Make sure all the plywood edges and the nail filler are sanded smooth. Prime the plywood edges first. When the primer is dry, sand the edges again, and prime the whole house. Again, sand any rough areas.

2 Carpenter Gothic houses tend to be painted rather conservatively, relying on their fancy trim to catch the eye. Still, that doesn't mean that you and your swallows might not enjoy some color contrast. At least paint the trim a different color from the house sides to show off your work!

PHOTO BY THOMAS STENDER

HOMETOWN EXUBERANCE

ROMANTIC ANTICLASSICISM AT THE BEGINNING OF THE NINETEENTH century produced the gothic novels of Mary Shelley and the Gothic Revival in architecture. The notion that a building should organically grow from within, rather than fit its uses and users into a golden rectangle, produced meandering floor plans and multi-facetted exteriors. Similarly, the idea that buildings should be expressive of emotion rather than stolidity resulted in flamboyant decoration derived from Gothic forms of the French, German, and English Renaissance. These influences produced a charming and relatively expensive, stone-fitted architecture, which still affects church design today. Translating the stone forms of the Gothic Revival into wood made the style available to builders of middle-class housing.

Two eerily like-named friends, Alexander Jackson Davis and Andrew Jackson Downing, popularized the Gothic Revival in America. They published books of plans and decorative patterns from which skilled carpenters could draw to produce varied houses for their clients. The recently developed balloon frame construction method allowed efficient building with standard-sized lumber. The invention of steam-powered scroll saws enabled carpenters to replicate intricate stone carving in the form of wooden "gingerbread." These three innovations conspired to let loose a torrent of house decoration that was distinctly American.

Despite the architects' Romantic theorizing about organic living spaces, the published floor plans tended to be rather simple and boxy. The exteriors of the houses told an entirely different story: Steep roofs were intersected with multiple gables and pierced by fancy chimneys, board-and-batten siding emphasized the vertical, scroll-sawn barge boards hung from eaves, and every window had molded hood trim. Bay windows and porches added to the profusion of shapes and seemed to invite additions, which only added to the charm of these houses. Soon, factory-sawn brackets, porch railings, and many shapes of shingles became available. In some instances, it seems that builders tried to use every shape available, all on the same house. Carpenter Gothic invited a response from the Moderns a century later by screaming, "More is more!"

DORIC TEMPLE
ROBIN HOUSE

ARCHITECT: Unknown

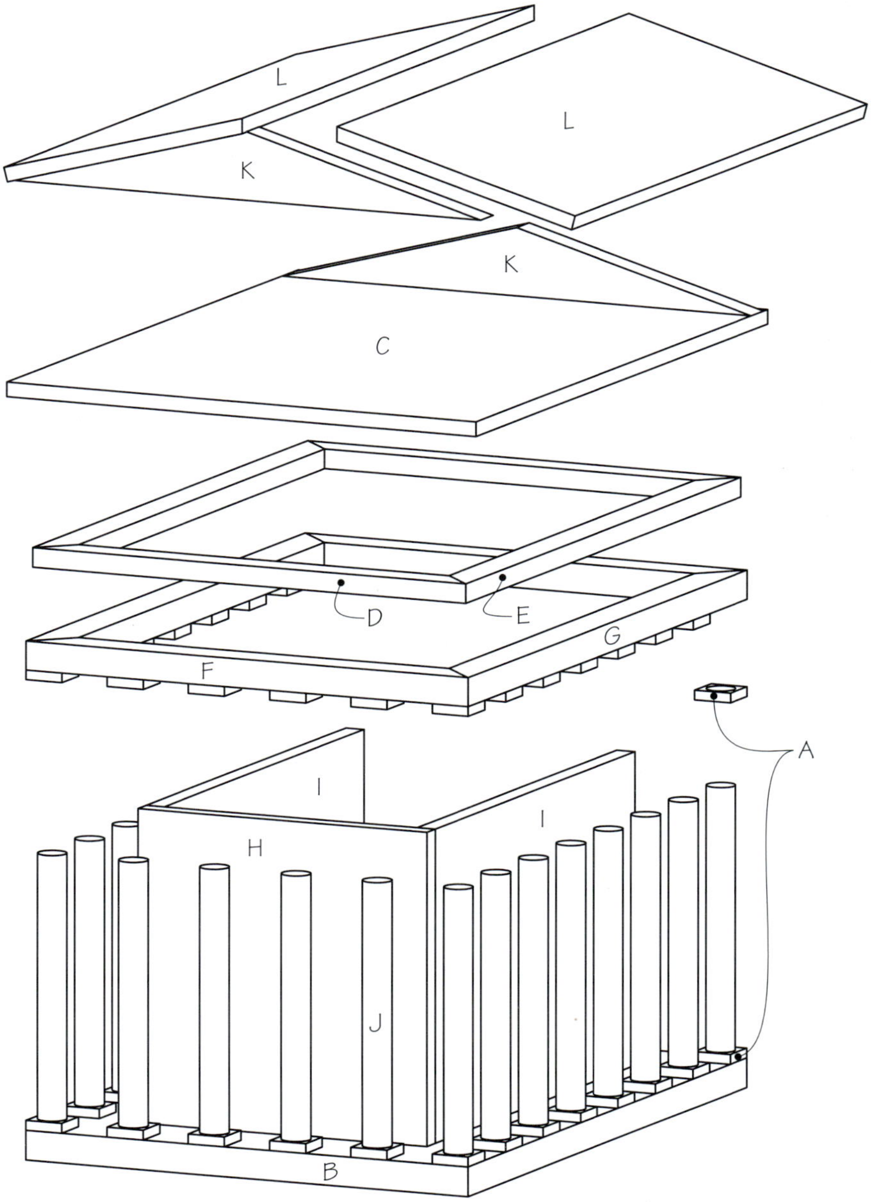

Although this temple incorporates none of the eye-fooling subtleties that distinguish its Greek models, at least it shares one important feature with them—its unadorned main room. And it's appropriate that the entrance is in the rear, because all robins ask is a roof over their heads and a nice view from their nest. This project is easy to build, especially if you get some help with its assembly.

CUTTING LIST

CODE	DESCRIPTION	QTY.	MATERIAL	DIMENSIONS
A	Bases and abacuses	40	plywood	1/4" x 1" x 1"
B	Floor	1	plywood	3/4" x 12 1/4" x 16 3/4"
C	Cornice	1	plywood	3/8" x 13" x 17 1/2"
D	Short friezes	2	pine	1/2" x 7/8" x 12"
E	Long friezes	2	pine	1/2" x 7/8" x 16 1/2"
F	Short architraves	2	pine	3/4" x 1" x 12 1/4"
G	Long architraves	2	pine	3/4" x 1" x 16 3/4"
H	Short wall	1	plywood	1/2" x 8" x 8"
I	Long walls	2	plywood	1/2" x 8" x 12"
J	Columns	20	beech	3/4" dia. x 7 1/4"
K	Tympanums	2	plywood	3/4" x 1 1/2" x 13"
L	Roofs	2	plywood	3/8" x 6 7/8" x 17 1/2"

MAKING THE BASE AND CORNICE ASSEMBLIES

1 We'll begin by making the pieces into which the columns will fit. Cut the bases and the abacuses (A), which are the pieces at the top of the columns that correspond to the bases below.

2 Cut the floor (B). Mark the positions for the bases, as detailed in figure 2, then glue them in place, flush with the edges of the floor. You can use spring clamps to hold them, but be careful not to pull the bases out of position.

3 Cut the cornice (C).

4 Prepare stock for the friezes (D and E) and the architraves (F and G). Miter the ends of these pieces, as shown in figure 3. The architraves should make a rectangle the same size as the floor, and the inside edges of the friezes should match those of the architraves. Use the floor to help mark the lengths of these pieces.

MATERIALS

1/4" exterior plywood, from scrap
3/8" exterior plywood, 1/4 sheet
1/2" exterior plywood, 1/8 sheet
3/4" exterior plywood, 1/4 sheet
Pine, 1 x 6 x 3'
5 dowels, 3/4" x 36" long

SUPPLIES

3d finishing nails
#6 x 1 5/8" decking screws
1/16" drill bit and 3/4" Forstner bit
#6 pilot bit

5 Glue the friezes to the cornice, ½" inside its edges. Glue the architraves to the friezes, with an even overhang all the way around, as shown in photo 1.

6 Mark the positions for the abacuses on the architraves, using the same spacing as for the bases. Then glue the abacuses in place, as shown in photo 2. Hold each one until the glue begins to set.

7 Use diagonal lines to mark the center of each base and abacus. Clamp a fence to the table of your drill press, ⅛" from the edge of a ¾" Forstner bit mounted in the chuck. (A Forstner bit is best for cutting holes in the small squares of plywood because it is less likely to tear the short-grain areas of the plies.) Feed the bit slowly through the layers of plywood. The setup is shown in photo 3. Drill a 9⁄16"-deep hole through each base and abacus.

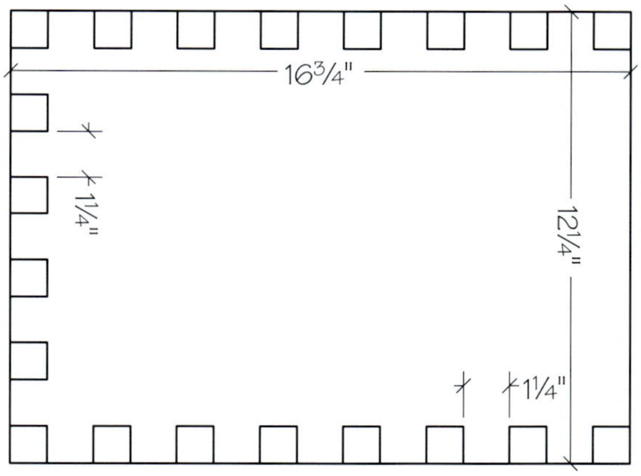

FIGURE 2. **Floor Layout**

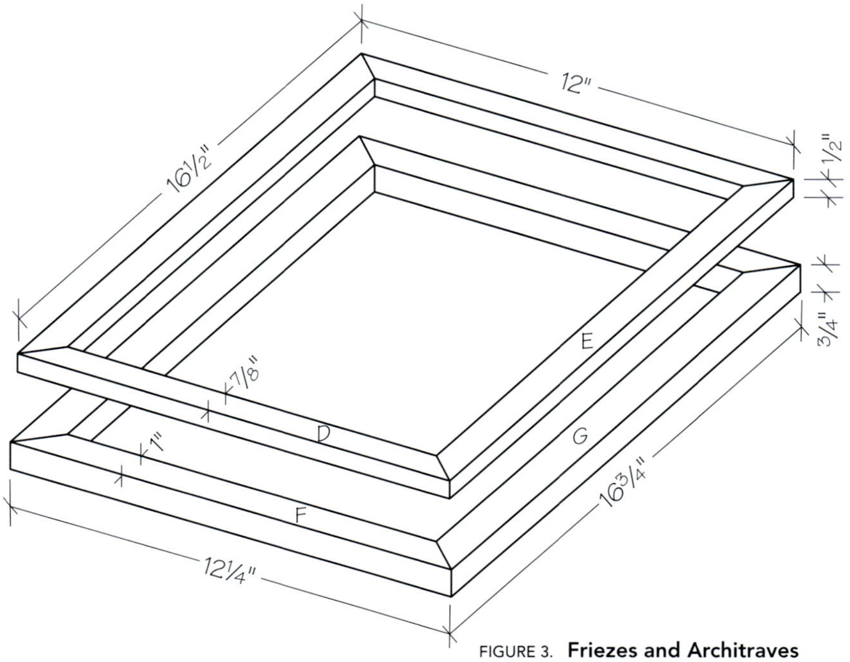

FIGURE 3. **Friezes and Architraves**

PHOTO 4

PHOTO 5

PHOTO 6

PHOTO 7

ASSEMBLING THE TEMPLE

1 Cut the walls (H and I). Apply glue to the front edges of the long walls, and clamp the short wall flush with their outside faces, as shown in photo 4. Drill angled 1⁄16" pilot holes, and fasten the walls with 3d finishing nails. Make sure that the joints are square.

2 Place the walls on the base as indicated in figure 4 (see page 48), and trace them. Flip the walls onto the underside of the cornice. Measure from the outside edges of the architraves to position the walls, and trace the outline of the walls on the cornice.

3 Drill #6 pilot holes within the marked areas through the base and the cornice. Countersink the holes from the opposite sides of the base and cornice, as shown in photo 5.

4 Glue the bottom edges of the walls and clamp them in place on the base. Extend the pilot holes into the walls, and fasten the walls to the base with screws (see photo 6).

5 We'll need all the help we can get when it's time to assemble the temple with all those columns, so we should drill some pilot holes now. Put the cornice assembly in place on top of the walls. Use a framing square to check the alignment of the base and the architrave, then extend the pilot holes into the top edges of the walls. Maintain accuracy by drilling one hole, driving that screw, and then extending the rest of the holes. Remove the screw and the cornice assembly.

6 Cut the columns (J) to length, using a stop on the miter gauge of your table saw. Make sure they fit easily into their holes, and sand them if necessary.

7 It's time to dance the colonnade, so find a partner! We've allowed 1⁄16" clearance for glue at each end of every column, but don't use so much glue that it squishes out all over the place. We're really relying on the glue and screws in the walls to hold the temple together. Begin by putting some glue in each of the holes in the base, then put a column in each hole. Run a line of glue on the top edges of the walls, and put a few drops on top of each column, as shown in photo 7. Hold the cornice in one hand while you use another hand to line up the back column on one side with its hole, and get the next column started with your "third" hand, and so on until all the columns are in their holes (see photo 8). Make sure that the walls match the traced lines on the cornice, and drive the screws to hold everything together. Wipe up the glue your partner dribbled.

PHOTO 8

PHOTO BY DENNIS THOMPSON, SICILY, ITALY

TO HONOR THE GODS

AS SOON AS THE GREEKS BEGAN BUILDING TEMPLES TO THEIR gods in the sixth century B.C., they made them large. The Ionic Temple of Artemis at Ephesus had columns 65 feet tall. Within 100 years, they had also become extremely refined. Of the three classical orders, the Doric seems the most straightforward, but a careful examination reveals that the viewer was considered in every sightline. The most obvious visual treatment was *entasis*, the gradual thickening and then thinning of the fluted columns as they rose from the base, which prevents them from appearing narrow-waisted, as straight columns do. Pronounced, even exaggerated in early Doric temples, entasis soon became almost unnoticeable.

A number of other, very subtle adjustments helped to achieve the same results, producing temples—large as they are—that feel light and entirely stable, offering no jarring visual moments. For instance, to balance their tendency to diminish when seen against the sky, corner columns are slightly thicker. Similarly, while the platform on which they stand is slightly higher in its middle, the columns themselves lean a little toward the inside. The columns seem to support the entablature and roof effortlessly.

The space between the columns and the temple proper, the *peristyle*, simply marks the sacredness of the rooms within, setting them apart from the ordinary world. In fact, the temples seem to have had little ceremonial purpose. Typically, they had two rooms, a treasury room in the back and the *cella*, the seat of the god, left unadorned except for a simple image. Although the temples were often situated amid spectacular scenery, their overall effect remains entirely self-referential, both calling attention to and denying their obvious immensity. They imitate the mystery of the gods they honor.

ADDING THE ROOF

1 Lay out the roof lines for the tympanum (K) on one blank, using the information in figure 5. Stack two pieces with their bottom edges aligned, and tape them together. On the band saw, cut the roof lines of both tympanums at once. These pieces must end in feather edges to allow the roofs to contact the cornice. After sawing, straighten the sawn edges with a belt sander.

2 Glue the tympanums to the cornice, ¼" back from its ends, and clamp them in place, as shown in photo 9. Use a ruler to make sure that the peaks are equidistant from the edges of the cornice.

3 Cut the roofs (L) to length, and bevel one long edge of each with the table-saw blade tilted to 14°, but leave extra width. Put the roofs in position, mark them so that you can return each to its side, and trace the edge of the cornice onto the underside of the roofs. Saw to the lines and trim the sawn edges with a low-angle block plane.

4 Lay the roof pieces on your bench, tops up, with their bevelled edges tight together. Tape across the joint to hold it while you attach the roof to the temple. Apply glue to the edges of the tympanums, just inside the edges of the cornice, and to the bevelled edges of the roof. Hold the roofs in place with spring clamps along their outside edges, making sure that the seam is tight along the peak. Drive 3d finishing nails through pilot holes to fasten the roofs to the tympanums.

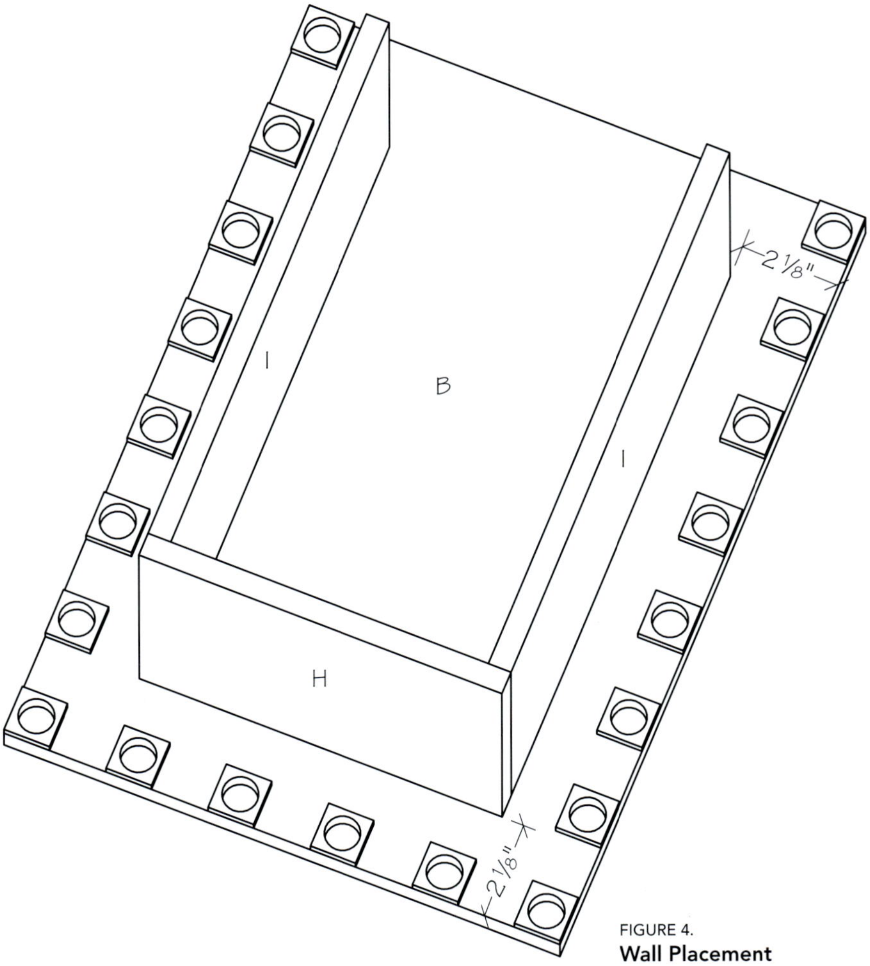

FIGURE 4. **Wall Placement**

PAINTING THE TEMPLE

1 Prime all the exposed plywood edges. When the primer is dry, sand it with 150-grit sandpaper, and prime the whole temple. Then sand everything again.

2 Paint your temple a warm marble color, or use multiple colors for an ironic, postmodern look (which just may be closer to its original color scheme).

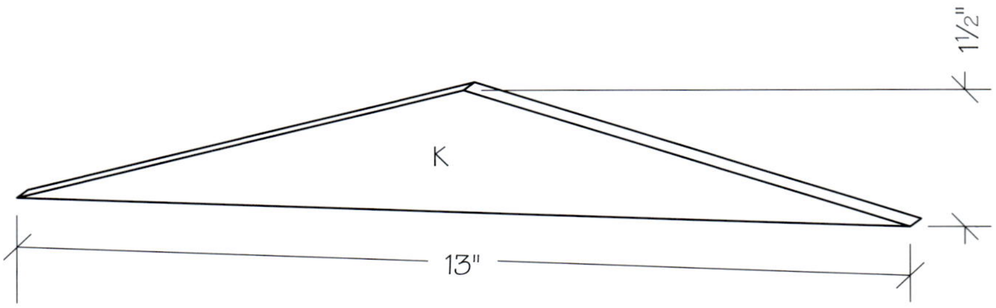

FIGURE 5. **Tympanum**

ARTS AND CRAFTS

FINCH BUNGALOW

ARCHITECT: Vernacular

Here's a house for the Finch family that incorporates all the features of a classic bungalow: a single story, a relatively flat roof, a porch, and, of course, an informal floor plan with the entrance opening directly into the living room, which is in turn barely differentiated from the dining room. Bungalows were intended to be easy to build, as is this one, but their exposed beams and knee braces, and their multiple roofs, posed special construction problems. One wag judged them "the least house for the most money." We've worked out the cutting difficulties, so you should have little trouble building this cozy house, which complements any site, from city lot to rural acreage.

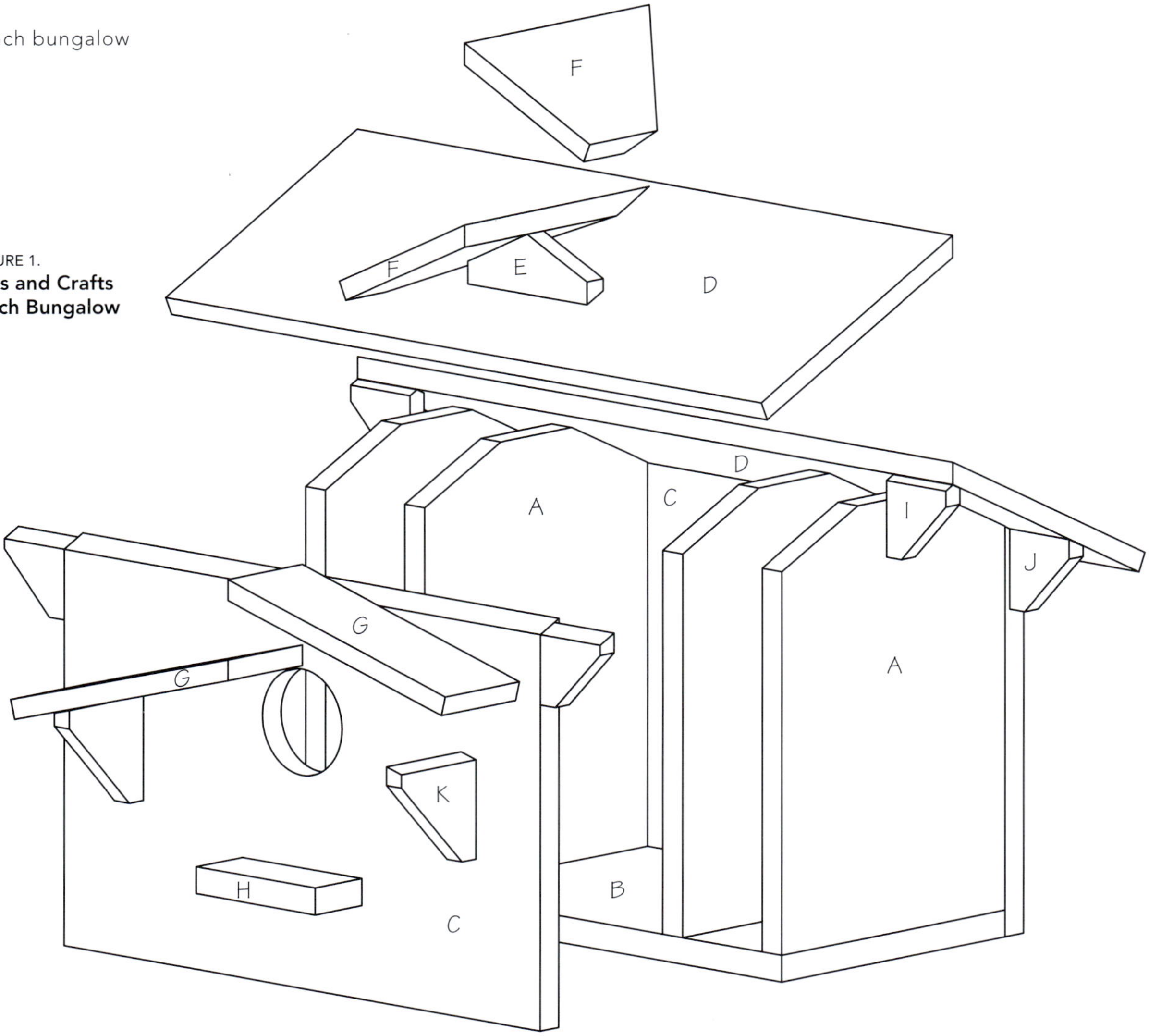

FIGURE 1.
Arts and Crafts Finch Bungalow

CUTTING LIST

CODE	DESCRIPTION	QTY.	MATERIAL	DIMENSIONS
A	Ends and partitions	4	plywood	1/2" x 6" x 8 1/8"
B	Floor	1	plywood	1/2" x 6" x 12"
C	Front and back	2	plywood	1/2" x 7 5/8" x 12"
D	Roofs	2	plywood	3/8" x 5 5/8" x 15"
E	Dormer end	1	plywood	1/2" x 1 1/8" x 3"
F	Dormer roofs	2	plywood	3/8" x 3 1/2" x 4 1/2"
G	Porch roofs	2	plywood	3/8" x 2" x 5 5/8"
H	Porch	1	plywood	1/2" x 1 1/4" x 3"
I	Peak brackets	2	plywood	3/8" x 1 1/2" x 1 1/2"
J	End brackets	4	plywood	3/8" x 1 1/2" x 1 1/2"
K	Front brackets	2	plywood	3/8" x 2" x 2"

PHOTO 1

PHOTO 2

PHOTO 3

BUILDING THE HOUSE

1 Cut the ends and partitions (A), using the dimensions in figure 2. Photo 1 shows how to cut the roof lines on the table saw using a stop with the miter gauge set at 25°.

2 Cut the floor (B), and square lines across its top face to mark the 6"-square nesting area shown in figure 3. Fasten the floor to the ends and partitions, using two screws per joint, driven through countersunk pilot holes, as shown in photo 2. The partitions land just outside the nesting area. Do not glue these joints; you'll need to remove the floor for yearly housecleaning.

3 Cut the front and back (C) pieces with 25° bevels on their top edges. Mark the center of the entrance hole on the front, as shown in figure 4. Bore the 2" hole on the drill press.

4 Square pencil lines across the inside faces of the front and back as you did on the floor, to help position the partitions. Spread glue on the front edges of the ends and partitions (but not on the floor). Clamp the front in place, drill angled 1/16" pilot holes, and drive 3d finishing nails to fasten the front, as photo 3 shows. Add the back in the same way. Set the nail heads. Remove the floor now, in case it needs some persuasion. If it fits too tightly for easy removal, plane its edges with a low-angle block plane.

MATERIALS

3/8" exterior plywood, 1/8 sheet
1/2" exterior plywood, 1/4 sheet

SUPPLIES

3d finishing nails
#6 x 1 1/4" decking screws
1/16" drill bit and 2" Forstner bit
#6 pilot bit

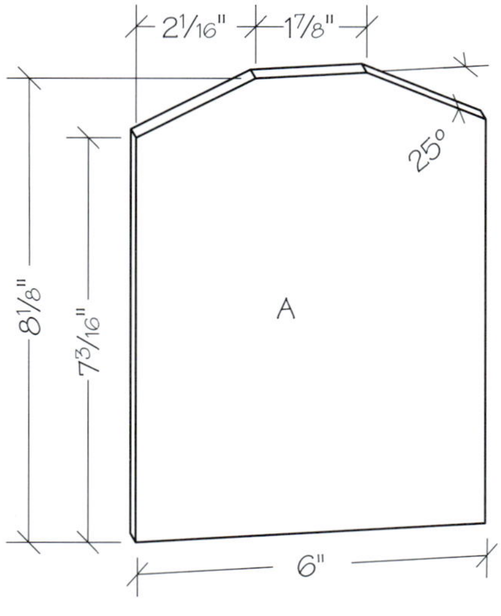

FIGURE 2. **Ends and Partitions**

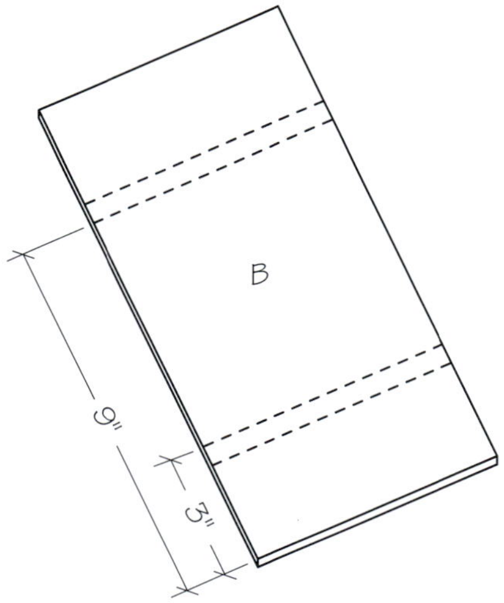

FIGURE 3. **Partition Positions on Floor**

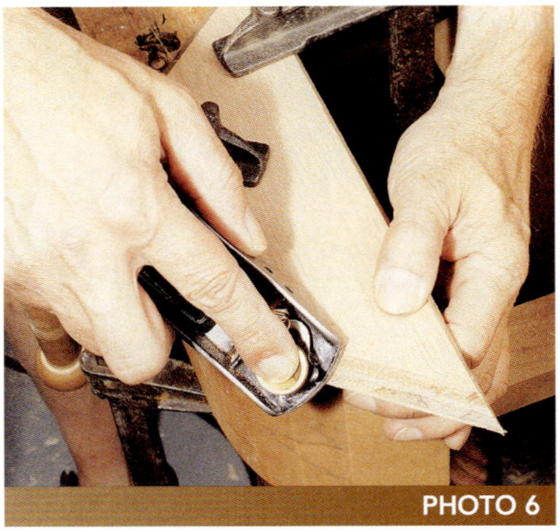

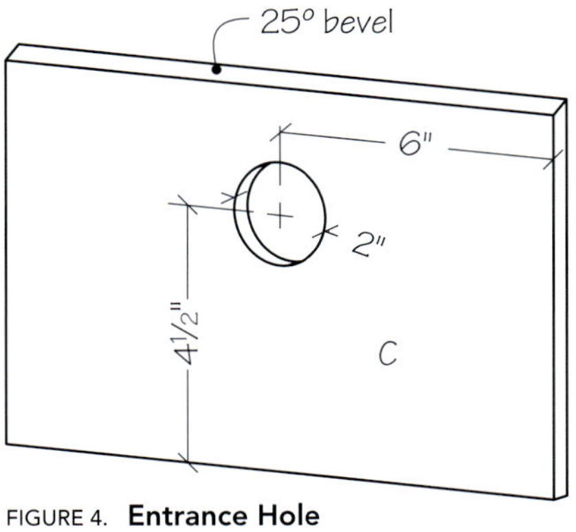

FIGURE 4. **Entrance Hole**

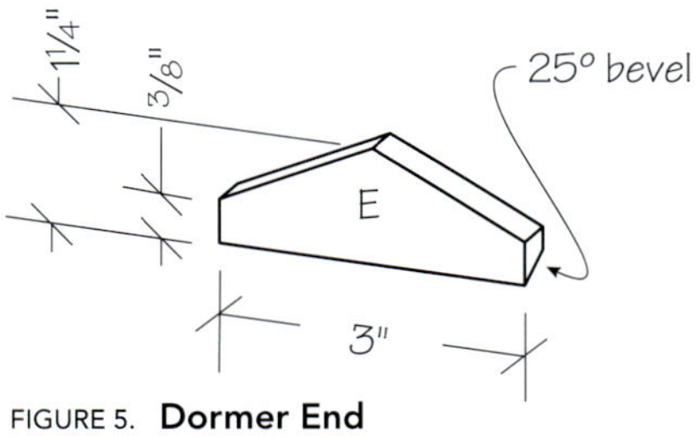

FIGURE 5. **Dormer End**

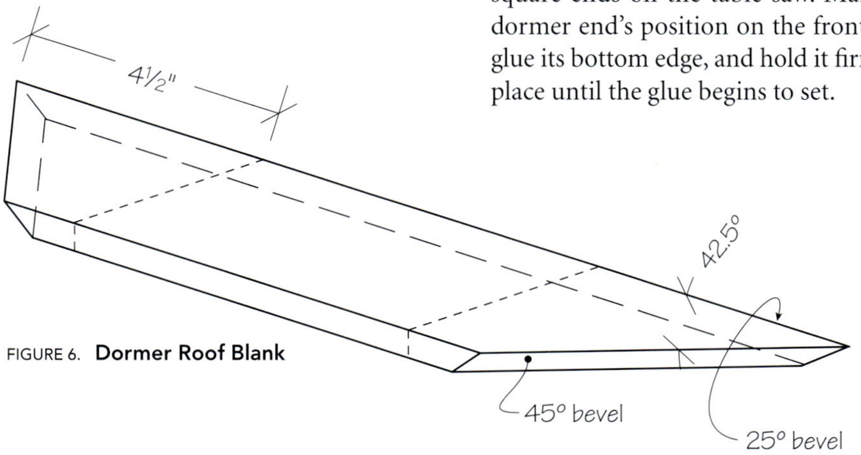

FIGURE 6. **Dormer Roof Blank**

5 Cut the roofs (D), with 25° bevels on their top edges. Mark the locations of the partitions on the roofs, to help position pilot holes. Lay the roofs on your bench with their pointed, peak edges together. Tape across this joint in several places, then carefully place the roofs on the house, with equal overhangs on the ends. Drill 1⁄16" pilot holes through the roofs into the ends and the partitions, as shown in photo 4. Remove the roof, so that you can apply glue to the edges of the ends and partitions, and to the bevelled edges of the roofs. Replace the roof, and fasten it with 3d finishing nails. Set the nail heads.

6 Follow figure 5 to cut the dormer end (E), with a 25° bevel on its bottom edge. Rip its bevelled edge first on an oversized piece of plywood. Then lay out the other lines. Cut the top edges with a band saw, jigsaw, or handsaw, and cut the square ends on the table saw. Mark the dormer end's position on the front roof, glue its bottom edge, and hold it firmly in place until the glue begins to set.

7 The dormer roofs (F) are the only tricky parts of this project, but here's a good way to cut them. Begin by cutting a 25° bevel on one edge of a 3½"-wide piece of ⅜" plywood about 15" long. With your table-saw blade tilted to 45° and the miter gauge set to 42.5°, cut opposing angles on the ends of the strip, as shown in photo 5. These cuts produce points at the bevelled edge of the strip and the end bevels (see figure 6). Unfortunately, the end bevels are not yet sharp enough. Cut a knife line parallel to, and 3⁄16" from, the bevel, on the bottom of the strip, as shown in photo 6. Clamp the strip to your bench and use a sharp low-angle block plane to increase the bevel angle until the bevel extends to the scribed line. Avoid planing all the way to the sharp corner of the bevel. Finally, cut square across the strip, 4½" from each point.

PHOTO BY RICHARD HASSELBERG, BLACK MOUNTAIN, NC;
RESIDENCE OF DONA CAVANAGH, ASHEVILLE, NC

BUNGALOW STYLE

THE BUNGALOW BUILDING BOOM IN THE UNITED STATES lasted from about 1890 until the Depression. Partly in reaction to Victorian excess, bungalow style drew on a variety of influences. The Arts and Crafts movement, Craftsman style, Japanese tea houses, Prairie style, adobe Spanish style, the informal plans of the Shingle style, and rural English cottages—all added a note or a chord to this distinctive style, with popular variations throughout America.

The ideal bungalow, as outlined by Gustav Stickley, was "a house reduced to its simplest form." By the end of the nineteenth century, of course, those words suggested something different than they would have to a seventeenth-century builder of Cape Cod houses. Stickley and other designers, such as Elbert Hubbard and Charles and Henry Greene, revered craftsmanship and truth to materials, as well as a more "honest," informal lifestyle. The resulting houses featured exposed structures, low-pitched roof lines, broad porches, and more open floor plans than had been popular before. Cobblestone foundations and chimneys, dark-stained beams and braces, and weathered shingles all remind us of the builder as we view the building. The bungalow style added several new expressions to the language of domestic architecture. Overhanging roofs and square, tapered porch posts were the most obvious of these, but the addition of a semi-public "stoop" in front of the semi-private porch had a more subtle effect on neighborhood life.

While skilled architects designed fine examples of the bungalow style, popular magazines published plans that any builder could use and change to fit local conditions or the owner's pocketbook. Sears, Roebuck & Company offered several bungalows through its mail-order catalog. All the necessary parts from the foundation up arrived at the site as a ready-to-assemble kit. These developments inevitably diluted the honest-craftsman intentions of the bungalow's theorists while keeping at least some of their stylistic traits. Even so, bungalows were not inexpensive because their single-story plans called for larger foundations, and the houses were full of architectural details. The Crash of 1929 effectively ended the building of middle-class bungalows, which, despite their professed simplicity, were still relatively showy. When domestic building resumed in earnest after the Second World War, it concentrated on the more efficient Cape Cod and ranch styles.

PHOTO 7

8 Hold the dormer roofs in place against the roof and the dormer end. They fit perfectly, don't they? You should at least have pretty good glue joints. Tape across the peak joint to help hold the two halves together. Glue up all the mating edges, and hold the assembly firmly in place until the glue begins to set. Wait a few more minutes before tapping 3d nails through pilot holes in the dormer roofs and into the dormer end. Set the nail heads.

9 Cut each porch roof (G) with a 15° bevel on one end. Mark each one's position on the front, just above the entrance hole. Tape across the bevel joint. Cut the porch (H), and mark its position 1¼" from the bottom edge of the front. Apply glue to the top bevel of the porch roof and to its back edges, and hold the roof in position for a minute. Spread glue on the back edge of the porch and hold this piece in the same manner as the porch. Then clamp both the porch and porch roof, as shown in photo 7, using scrap levers to extend your clamps.

10 Take a look at the brackets (I, J, and K) in figure 7. You'll see that they are easy to make if you bevel the top edges first, then cut them into squares, and finally cut the angle crossing the bottom corner. So go ahead and cut them. Just remember that the peak brackets (I) have bevels on both sides to fit against the underside of the roof peak, and that you need to make "right" and "left" versions of the other brackets.

11 Glue the brackets in place, as shown in figure 1. There—you're ready for some finishing fun.

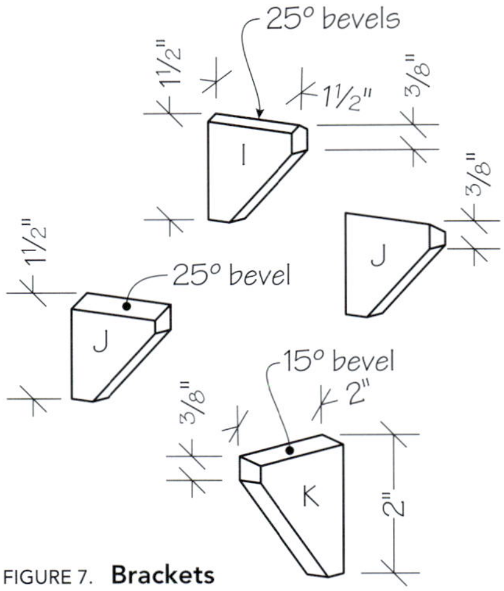

FIGURE 7. **Brackets**

PAINTING THE HOUSE

1 Replace the floor if you haven't already done so. Sand all the edges, and round their corners slightly. Prime the plywood edges.

2 When the first coat is dry, sand the primed areas, and prime the whole house. Sand again to prepare a smooth surface for your paint.

3 I used a light putty color to suggest stucco on the walls and under the eaves. You can paint the edges of the roofs, the porch, and the brackets with a rich brown. Then use the same color to suggest wooden brackets and to run a line around the walls at the level of the porch roof ends. I used a darker brown for the roof.

SOUTHERN COLONIAL MARTIN HOUSE

ARCHITECT: Vernacular

Technically, this house should be called a Greek Revival Southern Plantation House, but the more recent realtor's term seems fitting for a structure so far from its antecedents. If your martins choose to spend sultry afternoons in the shade of their piazza, so much the better. After all, the porches on plantation houses were a local addition to the Grecian temple form. Although it looks complicated, construction of this martin house proceeds in a straightforward manner, and the house will certainly be a distinctive addition to your backyard.

CUTTING LIST

CODE	DESCRIPTION	QTY.	MATERIAL	DIMENSIONS
A	Second floors	2	plywood	½" x 6⅛" x 25½"
B	Divider	1	plywood	½" x 12½" x 25½"
C	Partitions	12	plywood	½" x 6⅛" x 6⅛"
D	First floor	1	plywood	½" x 12½" x 25½"
E	Ceiling	1	plywood	½" x 17½" x 25½"
F	End walls	2	plywood	½" x 12½" x 13"
G	Gables	2	plywood	½" x 5½" x 17½"
H	Pillars	10	pine	¾" x ¾" x 13"
I	Porches	4	plywood	½" x 2" x 26½"
J	Fronts	2	plywood	½" x 13 x 26½"
K	Roofs	2	plywood	½" x 11" x 27½"
L	Dormers	8	plywood	2½" x 3⅜" x 5⅝"

FIGURE 1.
Southern Colonial Martin House

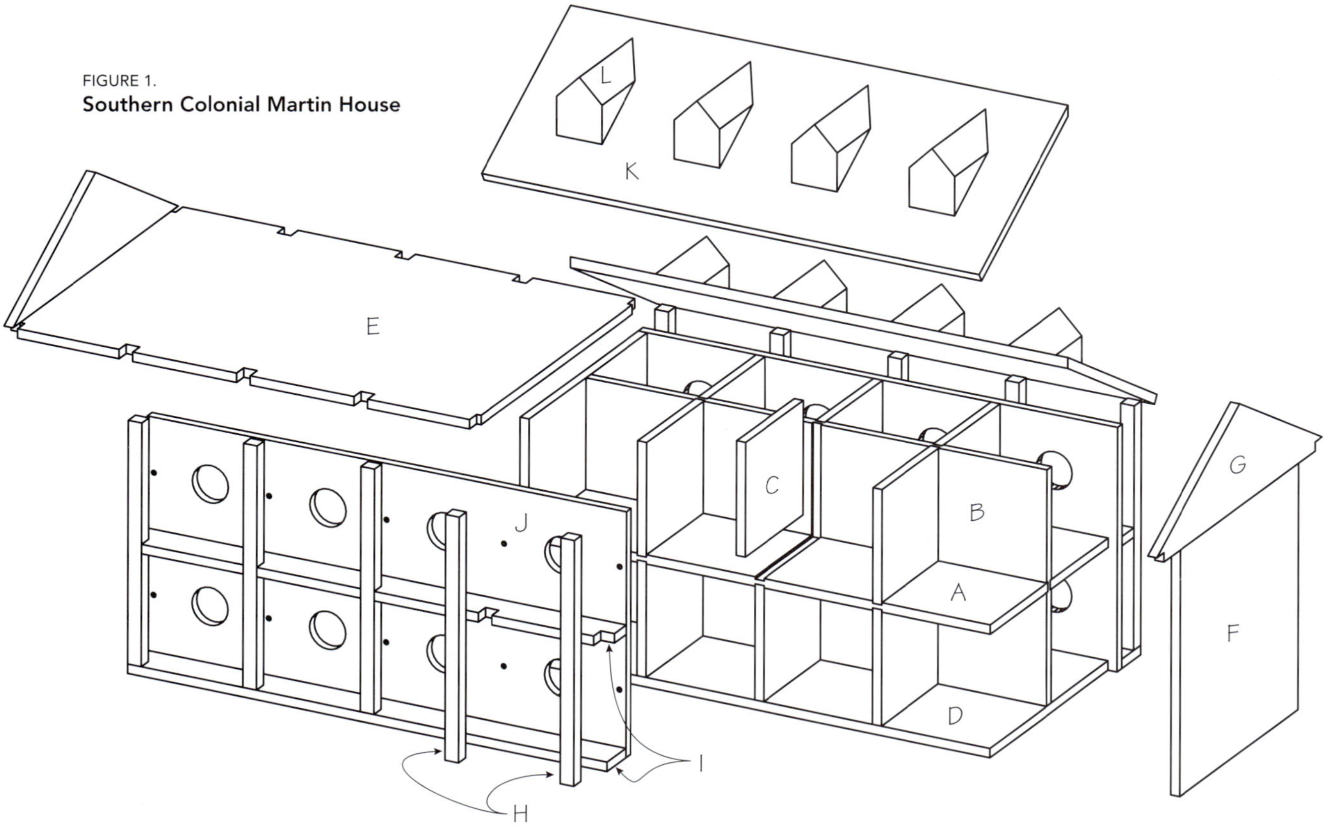

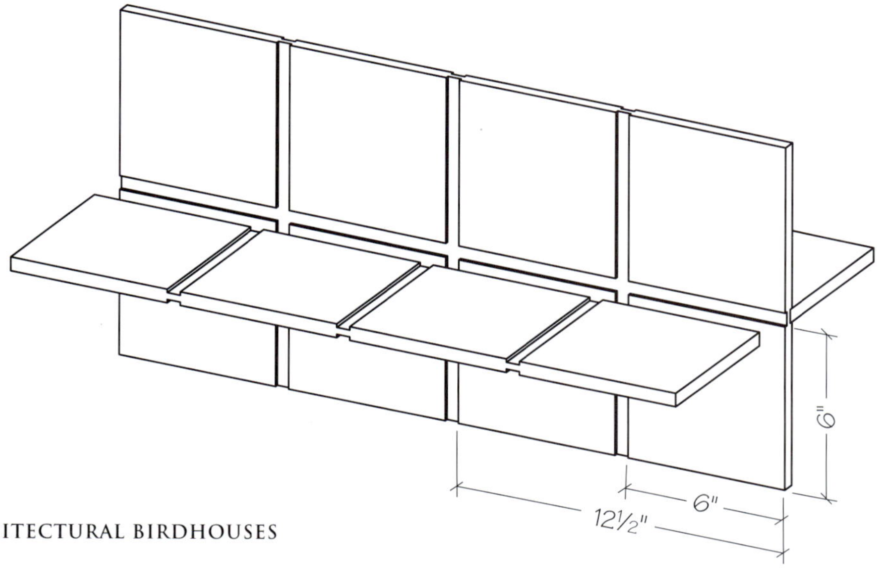

FIGURE 2.
Second Floors and Divider

ASSEMBLING THE ROOMS

1 We'll build the house from the inside out. Begin by cutting the second floors (A), divider (B), and partitions (C) to size on the table saw.

2 The divider and the floors are dadoed; then these parts and the partitions are held together with glue in the dado joints. Figure 2 shows the layout for the ⅛"-deep dadoes in both sides of the second floors and both sides of the divider. Adjust the width of your dado blade on the table saw for the thickness of the plywood you're using. Check the depth of the dadoes by cutting test dadoes on opposite sides of a piece of scrap plywood. Slide a partition into each dado, and measure the total length of the two partitions and the remaining core—it should measure 12". When the dado depth is correct, guide a long edge of the divider against the rip fence to center one dado on each side, as shown in photo 1.

3 Center opposing dadoes across the widths of the divider and the second floors, using a stop on the miter gauge, as shown in photo 2. Now you can cut all the remaining dadoes with one more setting of the stop, as photos 3 and 4 show.

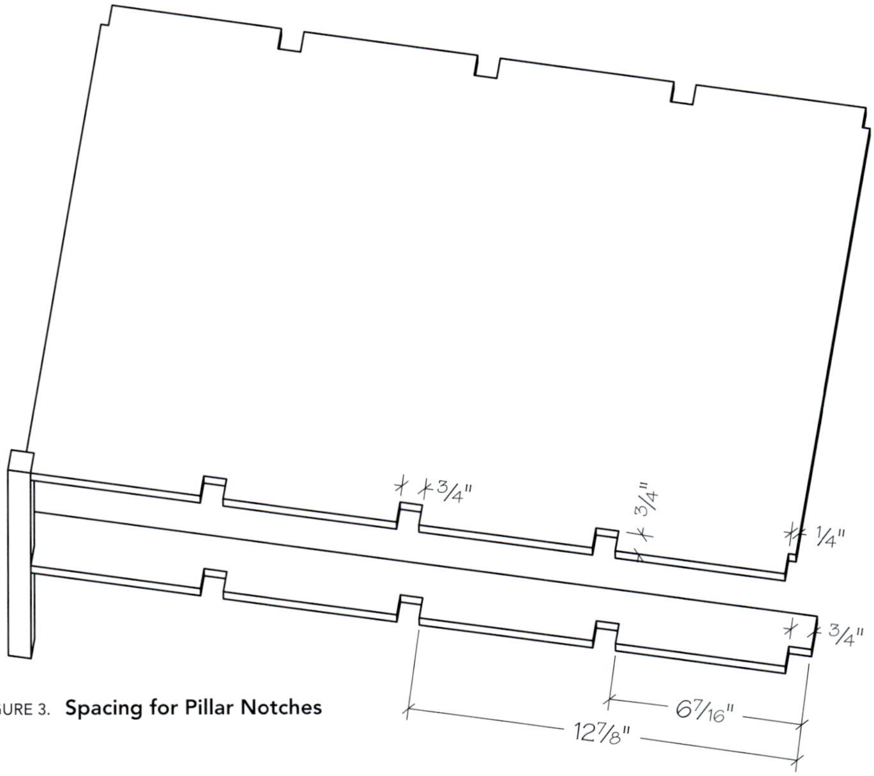

FIGURE 3. **Spacing for Pillar Notches**

PHOTO 1

PHOTO 2

PHOTO 3

PHOTO 4

MATERIALS

½" exterior plywood, 1 sheet

Pine, 1 x 4 x 5'

SUPPLIES

#6 x 1¼" decking screws

3d finishing nails

4d finishing nails

1⁄16" drill bit and 2¼" hole saw bit

#6 pilot bit

#20 biscuits

4 Lay the divider on your bench, run a line of glue into its dado, and press one second floor into place. The partition dadoes on the two pieces should line up. Glue two adjacent edges of each of six partitions, and press them into place. Use clamps as needed to hold the partitions until the glue dries, as shown in photo 5.

5 When the glue has dried, turn the assembly over to repeat step 4 with the remaining second floor and partitions.

6 Cut out the first floor (D). Stand the partition assembly on your bench so that a long edge of the divider is upward. The first floor should just fit on top of the divider and six partitions, with all the edges flush. Gather your 1/16" drill bit, drill, glue, hammer, and nail set. Throughout this project, you should drill angled, 1/16" pilot holes before fastening any joints with nails. To guide your pilot holes, draw lines on the first floor representing the centers of the edges of the divider and the partitions.

7 Remove the first floor, apply glue to the appropriate edges of the divider and partitions, and replace the floor. Clamp the floor to keep it from moving until you've driven a few nails. Nail the first floor to the divider and the partitions, driving two 3d finishing nails into each partition and eight nails, evenly spaced, into the divider.

8 Cut out the ceiling (E), the pillars (H), and the porches (I). Put two of the porches aside for now. The pillars run from the first-floor porches through notches in the second-floor porches and in the ceiling, as shown in figure 3. Cut all the notches now, before fastening the ceiling. Use a dado blade in your table saw, set to the thickness and depth of the pillars. You can use setups similar to those you used for the dados, except that the porches and ceiling will be held on edge against the miter gauge. Stack one porch in front of each edge of the ceiling to limit tearout to the upper side of the ceiling. You can cut the 1/4"-wide end notches with a stop, too, as shown in photo 6.

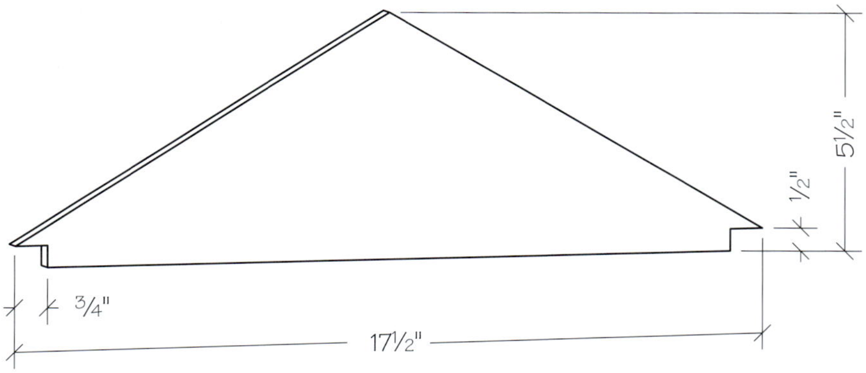

FIGURE 4. **Gable**

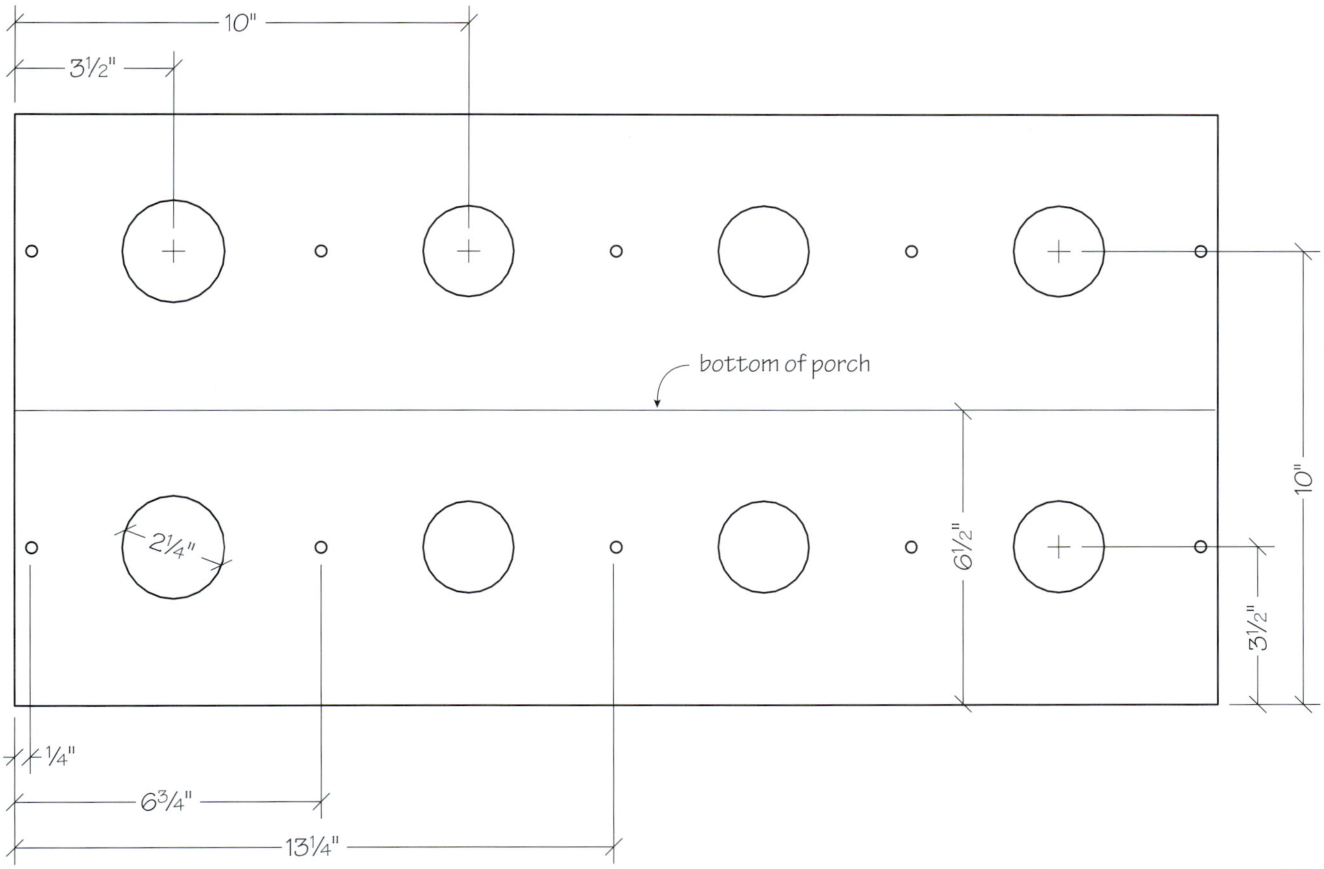

FIGURE 5. **Front**

9 To fasten the ceiling in place opposite the first floor, apply glue to the edges of the partitions and the divider, then position the ceiling so that its front and back overhang the partitions by 2½". Clamp the ceiling in place while you drive 3d finishing nails as before.

10 Cut the end walls (F) on the table saw. Lay out and cut the gables (G) on the band saw or with a jigsaw, according to the information in figure 4. Center the lower edge of each gable on the top edge of an end wall, and mark across the joint at its center and about 2" from each side of the end wall. Use those index marks to cut biscuit slots in the gables and the end walls, as shown in photo 7. (You can join these pieces with grooves and a separate tongue, too, if you don't have a biscuit joiner, or you can hold them together with a piece of duct tape on their inside faces. No, I'm not kidding—it all depends on whether you want to be a respectable landlord or a slumlord.)

11 Glue the top edge of each end wall and put glue in the slots. Insert three biscuits, and push the gables and walls together, realigning the index marks. Clamp across the joints if necessary, but be sure to keep the end wall/gables flat by centering the clamp pressure and/or by clamping the pieces to a flat bench. Wipe off any excess glue, and, when the glue has cured, sand the joint smooth with 100- and 150-grit paper.

PHOTO 7

12 Glue and nail the end wall/gables to the divider, second floors, and first floor. Note that the bottom edge of the end wall is even with the bottom of the first floor, and the bottom edge of the gable is even with the bottom of the ceiling. The notches in the gables match the notches in the ceiling.

PHOTO 8

PHOTO 9

ADDING THE FRONTS

1 Cut the fronts (J). Follow figure 5 to lay out and drill the entrance holes. Draw a line on each front for the bottom of the second-floor porch. Mark and drill pilot holes for #6 screws, one per partition, and similarly-spaced holes at the ends, as shown in photo 8. Note: The perceptive reader will see that the entrance holes in the photograph are considerably smaller than 2¼". I screwed up, okay? I had to go back later and redrill the holes to the correct size.

2 Find the porches. Trace the notches from a second-floor porch onto each of the unnotched porches. Glue a second-floor porch just above the line and an unnotched first-floor porch even with the bottom on each front. Reinforce the joints with 4d finishing nails driven from the insides of the fronts.

3 At each notch in a second-floor porch, apply glue, and push a pillar into place with its bottom end tight against the first-floor porch. Drive a 4d finishing nail at an angle through each pillar and into the second-floor porch. Drill pilot holes for #6 screws, and fasten the pillars to the first-floor porch, as shown in photo 9. Use a combination square to make sure the pillars are square to the porches.

4 Put each front in place against the edges of the house assembly. The top ends of the pillars fit into the notches in the ceiling. When the outside edges of the front are even with the floor and end walls, use an offset screwdriver to fasten the fronts with 1¼" screws. You will be able to remove the fronts to clean the apartments after each set of tenants moves out.

ADDING THE ROOF

1 Cut out the roofs (K) with a 30° bevel along their top edges, using the rip fence on your table saw.

2 Glue plywood into a stack 2½" thick for the dormers (L). Although it's somewhat wasteful of material, it's easiest to cut the "roof" bevels along one edge of the stack by using the table saw. Therefore, the stack needs to be 3½" wide and 48" long, but you can break up the length into any multiple of 6". Keep one edge of the stack flat and square, or make it so after the glue dries.

3 With that straight edge against the rip fence, cut 45° bevels on both sides of one edge, following the dimensions in figure 6 (see photo 10). Tape one of the cut-off wedges to the dormer blank to provide a marking surface for the next step, then trim the dormers to 5⅝" long.

4 Draw a diagonal line on each dormer, as shown in photo 11, and cut to the line on the band saw. Flatten the sawn face with a low-angle block plane or by rubbing the dormer on a sheet of sandpaper held flat on your bench.

5 Draw a line across each roof for the bottom edge of the dormers, and mark their locations, as indicated in figure 7. Glue one dormer at a time, and hold it in place until the glue begins to set, then move on to the next one. When the glue has dried, drill two #6 pilot holes through the roofs and into each dormer, and drive two 1¼" screws.

6 Before fastening the roofs, decide how to paint your house. You can spray the house as assembled so far, and paint the eaves and roof edges before you add the roofs. Fasten the roofs in place with glue and 4d finishing nails. Run a line of glue along the bevelled edge before you attach the second roof. When the glue has cured, drive 3d nails through the peak joint to reinforce it. You'll have to use the nail set to help drive the last little bit of nail.

PHOTO 10

PHOTO 11

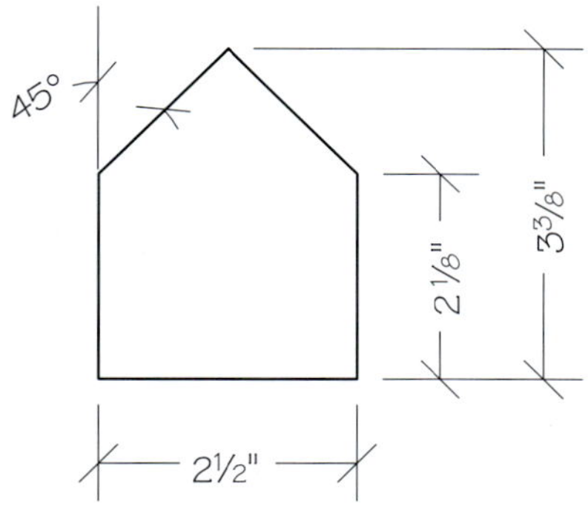

FIGURE 6. **Dormer End**

MAKE IT GREEK

PHOTO BY RICHARD AND CAROLYN BARNES, GREENWOOD PLANTATION, ST. FRANCISVILLE, LA

FOR MUCH OF THE EIGHTEENTH CENTURY, SUCCESSFUL AMERICAN colonists built houses in the Georgian style that was popular in England. Georgian architecture afforded them a perfect platform for showing their wealth. It was also the first house style to be recognized as such in America—Georgian buildings were designed by architects trained in England, not by your local carpenter. By the 1760s, American architects began to realize that continuing their pro-British bias did not agree with the prevailing political climate, and might, in fact, prove to be a poor career strategy. In reaction to Georgian opulence, and in congruence with the notions of democratic self-governance, the distinctly American, Federal style emerged. Still symmetrical, Federal architecture was much less ornamental than Georgian, stressing dignity and restraint instead. These were forthright buildings that presented their broad, relatively simple fronts to the world.

Ironically, the same political impulses that encouraged the Federal style also led to its antithetical successor. Soon after the Constitution was written, Americans began to identify their new democracy with the ideals of the ancient Greeks. Appropriating the heroic and classical architectural forms of Greek temples seemed the perfect way to express America's idealistic confidence. The Greek Revival style started with mansions and public buildings in the new capital, Washington, D.C., but soon spread outward among the new states to become the longest-lived architectural style in the country.

Greek Revival became so popular that owners changed existing houses to reflect the new style. Since their gable ends present the most characteristic aspect of Greek temples, houses were actually rotated on their foundations to accommodate extended pediments and columns. As the style spread, it was adapted to local conditions and toned down to fit smaller pocketbooks. Wooden fluted pilasters with flattened capitals could be added to corners of farmhouses to suggest columns; small columns could be added to existing porches, and complete temple-like entrances, with pediments and columns, could be appended to houses built in the Federal style. In this way, Greek Revival became the normative style of domestic architecture until the end of the nineteenth century.

PAINTING THE HOUSE

1 Fill all the nail holes, and sand them smooth with 150-grit paper. Remove the front assemblies so that you can paint everywhere without adhering them to the house. You may be able to find white coated decking screws, which will be less noticeable when you reassemble the house.

2 Prime every exterior surface, and sand them thoroughly with 150-grit sandpaper when the primer has dried. You may find areas that need a second coat of primer. And a second sanding, of course.

3 Unless you're a total radical, choosing colors for this house will be pretty easy: Choose white. Archaeologists didn't discover until recently that the Greek temples were "polychromed," as they say when they mean "painted with many colors." So everyone painted their Greek Revival houses white to imitate the way the temples look today. The roof can be gray or aluminum-colored, because these houses often had tin roofs.

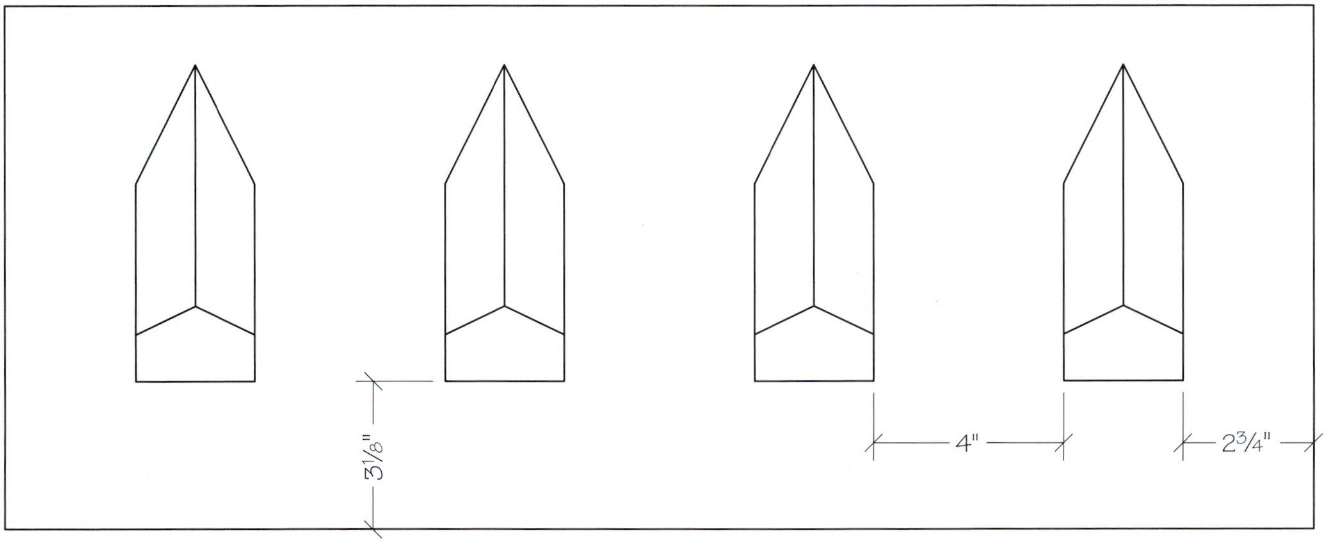

FIGURE 7. **Dormer Positions**

AT&T BUILDING
FINCH HOUSE

ARCHITECT: Philip Johnson

Tall buildings tend to occupy expensive land. Building upward increases the usable space on urban sites, making them economically feasible. But Philip Johnson has pointed out that hubris and corporate identity provide other compelling reasons for building skyscrapers. While birds may not care about architectural reknown, this icon of Postmodernism still makes a great home for your finch family. Like the original, it'll probably be the only one on your block.

PHOTO 1

BUILDING THE NESTING BOX

1 Cut the ceiling, divider, top linings, and floor (A–D). This project is fastened with glue and, where specified, finishing nails. Always drill 1/16" pilot holes for the nails, and, where possible, angle the nails for better holding power.

2 Glue and nail the divider (B) between the top linings (C), 6" from one end, as shown in figure 2. Use 4d finishing nails.

3 Glue and nail the ceiling (A) to the linings and the divider, as shown in figure 2, again with 4d nails.

4 Cut the sides (E). On one of the sides, bore a 2" entrance hole, centered widthwise and 3½" from the top of one side, as shown in figure 3. Lay out and cut the slots and holes on both sides, as detailed in figure 3. Drill a series of holes to remove most of the waste from the slots, then chop out the rest using a sharp chisel, as shown in photo 1.

MATERIALS
3/8" exterior plywood, 1/8 sheet
1/2" exterior plywood, 1/2 sheet
Pine, 1 x 8 x 4'
2" PVC pipe, 1'

SUPPLIES
3d finishing nails
4d finishing nails
1/16" drill bit and 2" hole saw bit
2 butt hinges, 1" x 1"
1" hook and eye
Clear silicone caulk

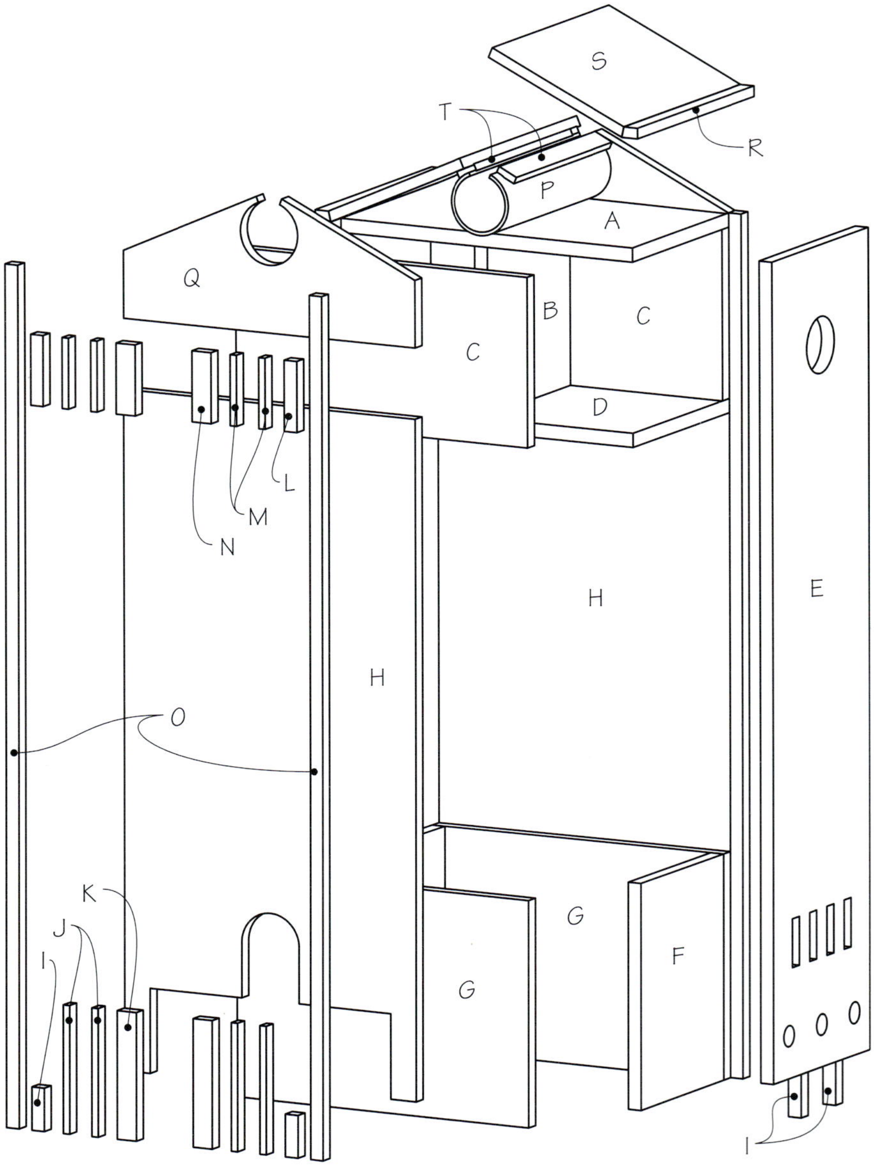

FIGURE 1. **AT&T Building Finch House**

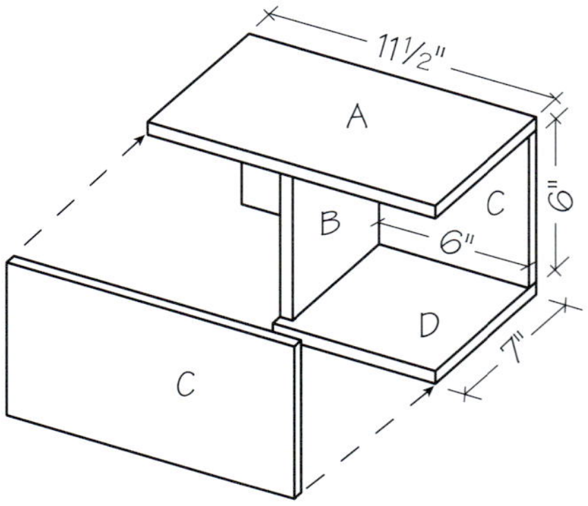

FIGURE 2. **Nesting Cavity**

CUTTING LIST

CODE	DESCRIPTION	QTY.	MATERIAL	DIMENSIONS
A	Ceiling	1	plywood	½" x 7" x 11½"
B	Divider	1	plywood	½" x 6" x 6"
C	Top linings	2	plywood	½" x 6" x 11½"
D	Floor	1	plywood	½" x 6½" x 6¹⁵⁄16"
E	Sides	2	plywood	½" x 7" x 29"
F	Side linings	2	plywood	½" x 6" x 8"
G	Bottom linings	2	plywood	½" x 8" x 11½"
H	Fronts	2	plywood	½" x 11½" x 24⅛"
I	Short piers	8	pine	½" x ½" x 1½"
J	Thin piers	8	pine	¼" x ½" x 4½"
K	Fat piers	4	pine	½" x ¾" x 4½"
L	Top side piers	4	pine	½" x ½" x 2½"
M	Top thin piers	8	pine	¼" x ½" x 2½"
N	Top fat piers	4	pine	½" x ¾" x 2½"
O	Long piers	4	pine	½" x ½" x 30½"
P	Cylinder	1	PVC pipe	2" diameter, 8" long
Q	Pediments	2	plywood	½" x 4¾" x 11½"
R	Side roofs	2	plywood	⅜" x ⅝" x 8½"
S	Roofs	2	plywood	⅜" x 5¾" x 8½"
T	Spacers	2	pine	¼" x ¾" x 7"

5 Glue and nail the side with the entrance hole to the edges of the linings and the ceiling. Put the floor (D) in place against the bottom edges of the linings and the divider. Install butt hinges to connect the floor and the side. Install a hook and eye to keep the floor in place, as shown in photo 2.

6 Glue and nail the other side to the opposite ends of the ceiling and the linings. Make sure that the edges of the two sides are parallel.

7 Cut the side linings (F) and the bottom linings (G). Glue and nail the bottom linings to the edges of the side linings, with their edges flush, as shown in photo 3.

8 Glue the lining box to the sides, with 1½" of lining extending beyond the bottom of the ends, as shown in photo 4. Apply the glue to the sides to avoid the holes and slots. Use plenty of clamps.

PHOTO 2

PHOTO 3

PHOTO 4

PHOTO 5

PHOTO 6

PHOTO 7

PHOTO 8

ADDING THE FRONTS AND PIERS

1 Cut out the fronts (H), using the information in figure 4. (This building has two identical fronts, unlike the original, which has only one fancy facade.) Use the band saw or a jigsaw to cut to the layout lines. Then clean up the sawn edges with a cabinetmaker's rasp and 100-grit sandpaper, but don't round those edges!

2 Glue the fronts, one at a time, to the linings, as shown in photo 5. Notice that the fronts don't touch the sides. Make sure that the bottom edges of the sides and the fronts line up. Clamp where you can.

3 Cut all the piers (I–O), and plane them to the thickness of your plywood. Follow the dimensions in figure 4 and figure 5 to glue all the piers except the long piers (O) to the linings. Make sure all the piers are vertical. Hold each pier firmly in place until the glue begins to set, as shown in photo 6.

4 Cut the plastic cylinder (P) to length. You can accomplish this safely with the miter gauge on the table saw if you feed slowly and hold on tight to keep the pipe from rolling. Then lower the saw blade until only ¼" is showing. Set the rip fence to one-half the diameter of the pipe, and saw through the pipe lengthwise, as shown in photo 7. Keep the heels of your hands firmly on the rip fence, and hold the pipe steady to cut a straight line. The pipe may want to collapse on itself, so be ready for a little extra friction near the end of the cut. If the pipe has completely closed the saw kerf, cut down the same line again. If this process makes you uncomfortable, cut the pipe with a handsaw.

5 Cut the pediments (Q) to their rectangular dimensions. Clamp one pediment in place atop the upper piers. On its top edge and inside face, mark a centerline. With the cylinder lying on the ceiling, butt one end against the pediment, and make sure that it's centered, as shown in photo 8. Trace the cylinder on the pediment with a sharp pencil. You'll have to remove the pediment and reposition the cylinder to finish the tracing. Use figure 6 as a guide in laying out the roof line on the pediment, but note that the roof angle may vary slightly depending on the diameter of your cylinder. Adjust the angle of the roof to leave a ¼" space between the cylinder and the top corner of the roof line.

6 Stack the pediment pieces, tape them together, and saw to the lines on the band saw or with a jigsaw. Smooth the roof lines with a low-angle block plane, and use a cabinetmaker's rasp to adjust the hole until the cylinder slides in easily.

7 Glue one pediment to the lining, and nail it to the edge of the ceiling. Run a bead of clear silicone caulk around the cylinder near each end, and slide the cylinder into place. Apply glue to the opposite lining, and slide the second pediment onto the cylinder and into place against the ceiling. Nail the second pediment to the ceiling as before. Clamp the pediments lightly, if necessary.

8 Glue and nail the long piers (O) in place at the corners.

9 Cut the side roofs (R) and the roofs (S), with 11° bevels on their meeting edges. Tilt your table-saw blade to 11°, and use the rip fence to guide the roof pieces.

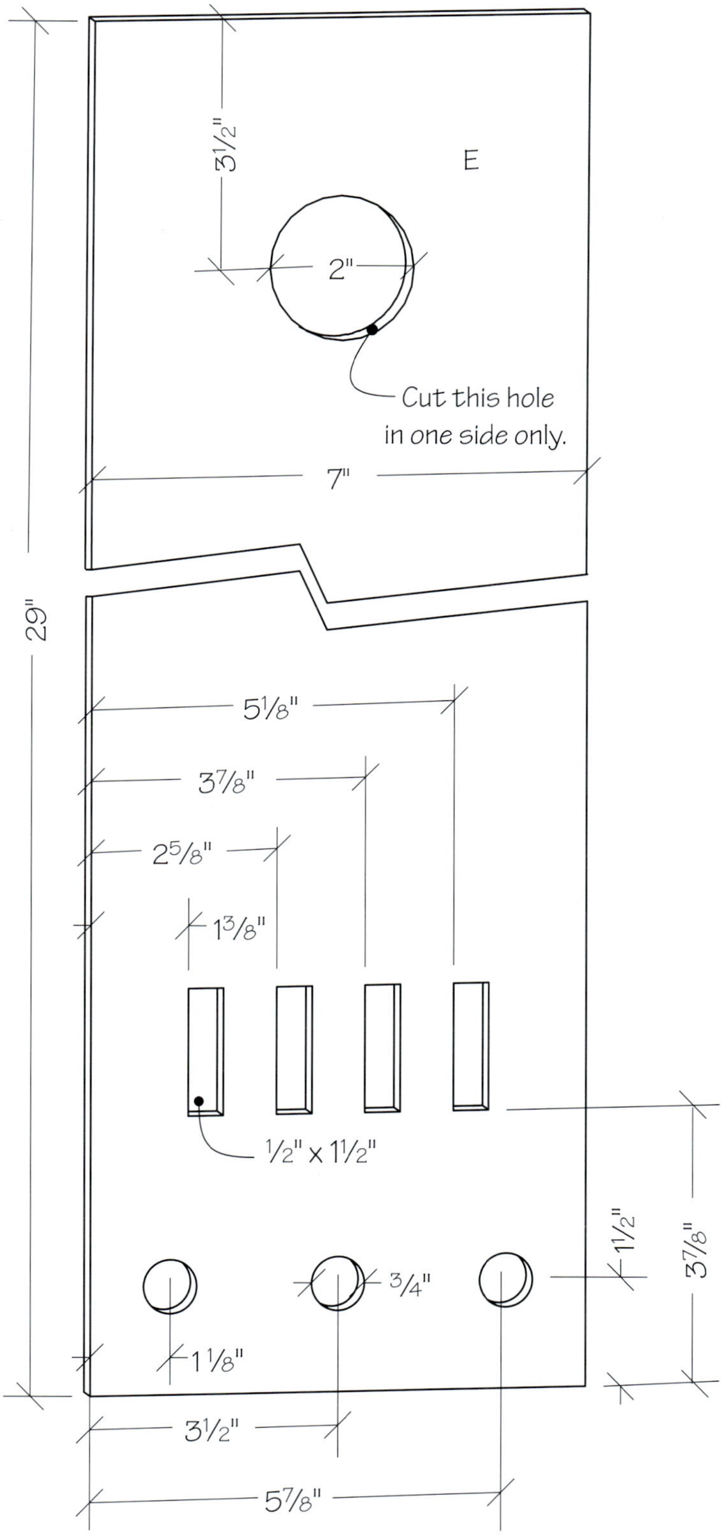

FIGURE 3. **Side Openings**

10 Cut the spacers (T), and glue them, centered along the roof edge, as shown in figure 1. When the glue has cured, put the roofs in place to check the fit. Plane the spacers, and clean up excess caulk where necessary, until the roofs fit tightly against the pediments.

11 Run a small bead of silicone caulk on the face of each spacer, then glue and nail the side roofs and the roofs in place, using 4d finishing nails.

12 When the glue and the caulk have cured, use a handsaw, guided by the roof edge, to cut away the extra cylinder, as shown in photo 9. Fill any gaps around the cylinder with silicone caulk.

PHOTO 9

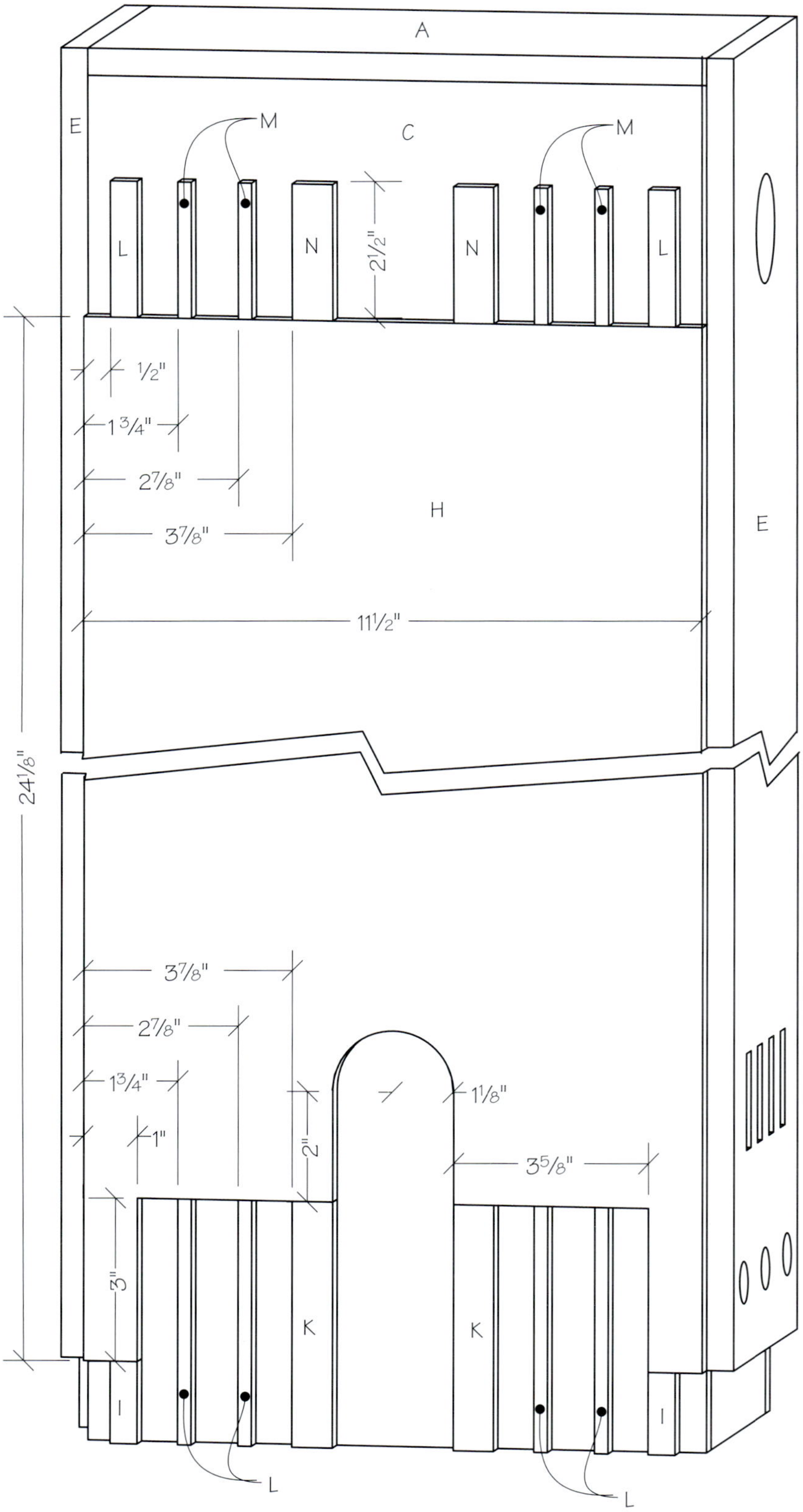

FIGURE 4. **Fronts and Front Piers**

LARGE-SCALE POSTMODERNISM

MORE A PERCEPTIVE READER OF THE CURRENT ZEITGEIST THAN A TRUE innovator, Philip Johnson has used his considerable talent and charm to secure his standing as one of the most influential architects in the United States. By the time he designed the AT&T Building with his partner, John Burgee, he had already reinvented himself several times. Johnson was the first director of the architecture department at the Museum of Modern Art in the '30s; built his Glass House in New Canaan, Connecticut, based on the ideas of Mies van der Rohe, in the '40s; aided Mies in the design of the Seagram Building in the '50s; and broke away from the rectilinear International Style in the '60s. He had just finished building Pennzoil Place in Houston when AT&T began searching for an architect for its New York City headquarters.

Johnson and Burgee nearly failed to apply for the commission in 1975, mistaking the formal inquiry for a request to update their promotional materials. Even so, their final presentation to the search committee consisted of two photographs—one of the Seagram Building and the other of the Pennzoil—and a line of charming chat. Architectural theorists had begun re-examining classical forms as an antidote to the steel-and-glass boxes of the International Style; appropriating the old was the new thing named Postmodern. In part, the postmodernists argued that historical references offered a more welcoming face in an urban context. Johnson obliged by designing a street-level arcade reminiscent of the Italian Renaissance, but blown up to a gigantic scale. Similarly, he faced the building with granite rather than glass. But what everyone remembers about the AT&T Building is its top.

PHOTO BY JEFFERY HOWE, BOSTON, MA

Aiming for monumentality, Johnson designed an abstracted broken pediment—a feature of Chippendale furniture already borrowed (and altered) from classical temples. Long before the building was completed in 1984, that crown attracted considerable attention, gratifying Johnson and, perhaps, his clients. The press debated whether this new architecture honored the past or made fun of it. Critics pointed out that the base of the building had nothing in common with its top, and that the shaft connecting them was uninspired. AT&T executives had wanted a headquarters equal to the Seagram Building, but different. They got "different," and the aesthetic deficiencies of their edifice were at least balanced by its notoriety.

PAINTING THE HOUSE

1 Sand the house thoroughly with 150-grit paper, especially the exposed plywood edges. Prime the edges twice and all other surfaces once, sanding after each coat.

2 Paint the lining areas a darker shade of the color you use for the outside of the building. I used a light reddish buff color to suggest the granite of the AT&T Building.

3 When the paint is thoroughly dry, mask around the windows with ¼", ½", and ¾" masking-tape lines (refer to the project photos). To produce the narrow lines, press on wider tape, and then cut it to size with a craft knife guided by a long ruler. Then paint the windows a warm medium gray. Remove the masking tape as soon as you've finished painting each side.

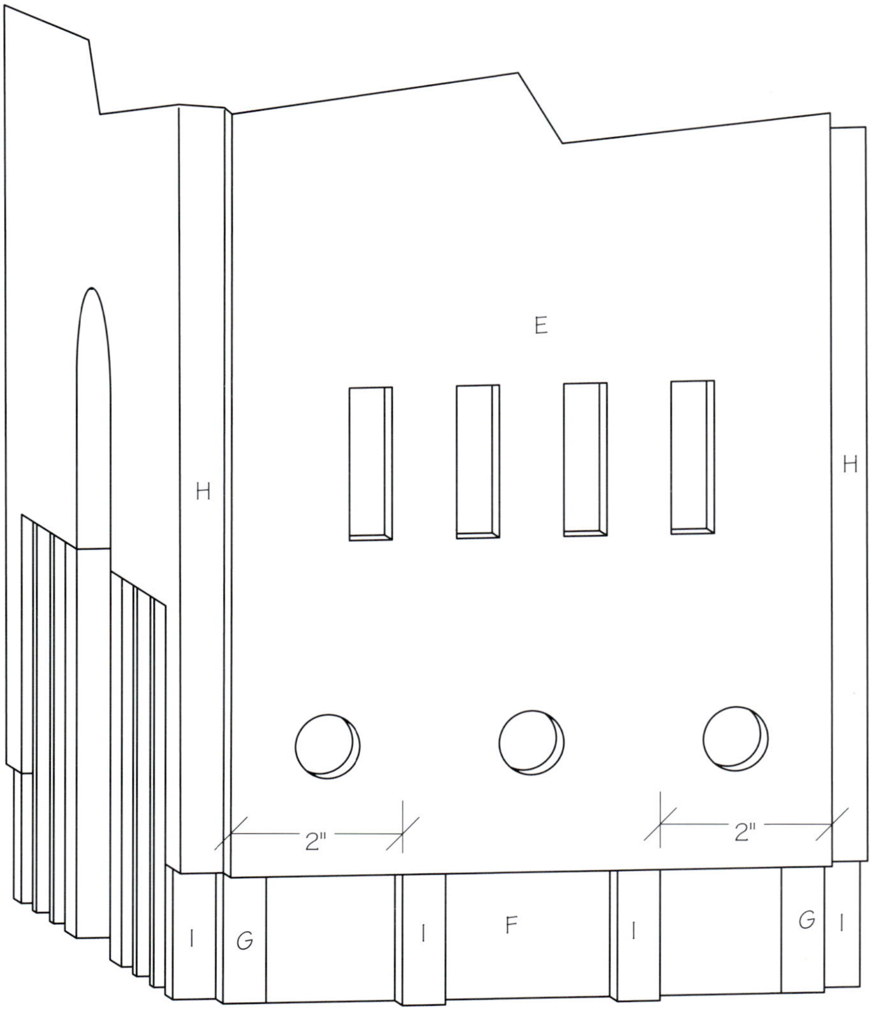

FIGURE 5. **Side Piers**

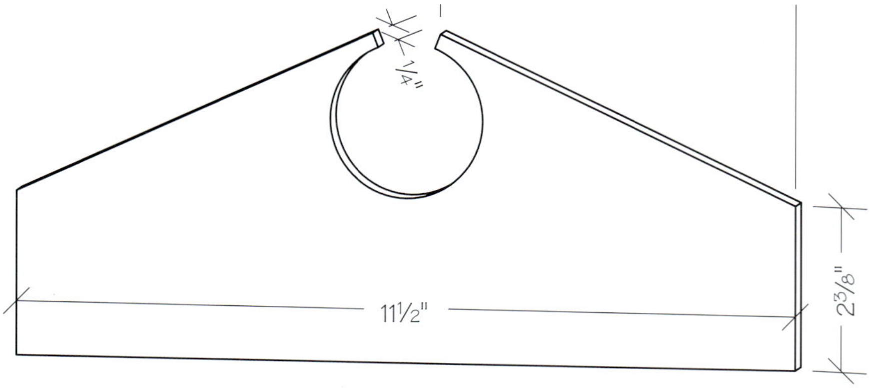

FIGURE 6. **Pediment**

TIKAL I
TITMOUSE HOUSE

ARCHITECT:
Mayan Master Stonemason

The steep stairway characteristic of Mayan pyramids was clearly intended to emphasize the difference in status between the worshipped beings and their subjects. Your titmice will experience no such difficulty of approach, making them appropriate residents of a temple. This project involves pattern routing and precision joinery, but the steps described here teach the value of meticulous planning. Follow them carefully to produce a near-scale model of the original.

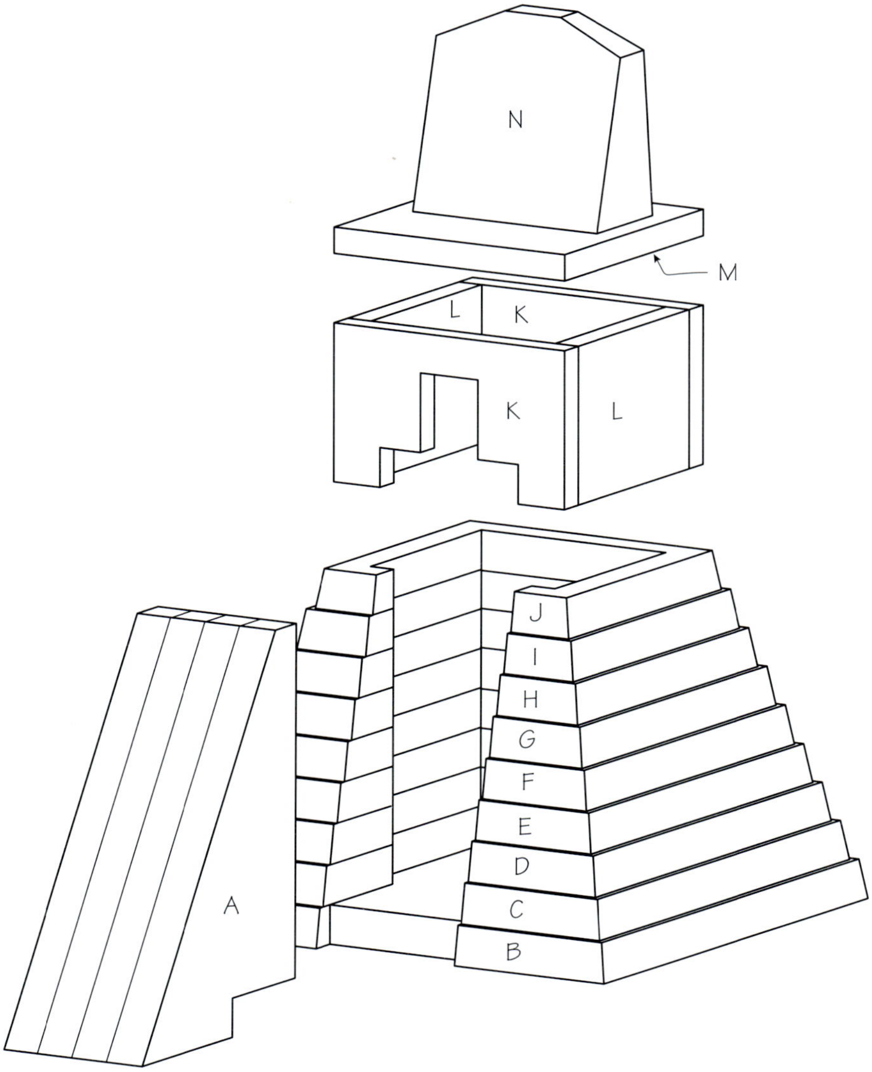

FIGURE 1. **Tikal 1 Titmouse House**

MAKING THE STAIRS AND LAYERS

1 Start with the stairs (A). Begin by gluing and clamping four pieces of ¾" plywood to make an oversize blank that's roughly 6" x 8". Take particular care to align the edges on one long side of the stack as you apply clamping pressure.

2 While the glue is drying, cut the nine layers of the pyramid (B–J) from ¾" plywood, making them all 9½" square and leaving their edges unbevelled. Stack the nine layers, and measure their total thickness. Use that measurement plus ¾" as the height of the stairs in the next step.

3 Plane off any excess glue from the flush edge of the stairs blank, then use that edge against the miter gauge on your table saw to crosscut the blank to finished length. The flush edge will be the back side of the stairs.

4 Lay out the taper on the stairs blank, as shown in figure 2. Saw to the line on the band saw. I left the saw marks rough to suggest the stone steps of the original pyramid.

CUTTING LIST

CODE	DESCRIPTION	QTY.	MATERIAL	DIMENSIONS
A	Stairs	1	plywood	3" x 5½" x 7½"
B	Layer 1	1	plywood	¾" x 9½" x 9½"
C	Layer 2	1	plywood	¾" x 9" x 9"
D	Layer 3	1	plywood	¾" x 8½" x 8½"
E	Layer 4	1	plywood	¾" x 8" x 8"
F	Layer 5	1	plywood	¾" x 7½" x 7½"
G	Layer 6	1	plywood	¾" x 7" x 7"
H	Layer 7	1	plywood	¾" x 6½" x 6½"
I	Layer 8	1	plywood	¾" x 6" x 6"
J	Layer 9	1	plywood	¾" x 5½" x 5½"
K	Front & back	2	plywood	½" x 3" x 5"
L	Sides	2	plywood	½" x 3" x 4"
M	Roof	1	plywood	½" x 5" x 5"
N	Crown	1	plywood	4" x 2" x 3¾"

MATERIALS

1/2" exterior plywood, 1/8 sheet
3/4" exterior plywood, 1/2 sheet

SUPPLIES

4d finishing nails
#6 x 1 1/4" decking screws
#6 x 1 5/8" decking screws
1/16" drill bit
1/2" ball-bearing flush-trimming router bit
#6 pilot bit
Double-sided (carpet) tape

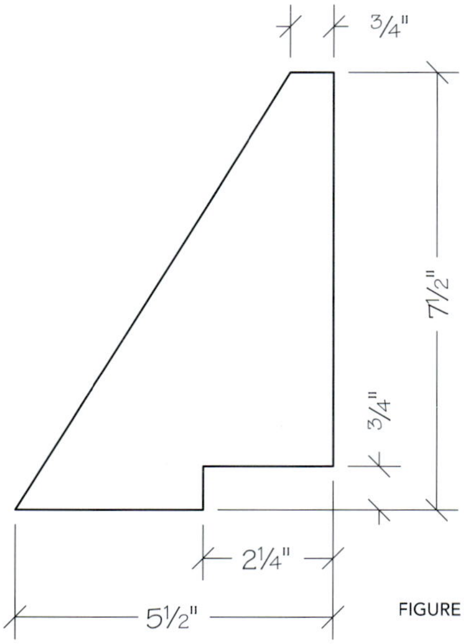

FIGURE 2. **Stairs**

5 Cut a ¾" x 2¼" notch from the bottom back corner of the stairs stack, as shown in figure 2. You can do this most easily on the table saw by setting the blade 2¼" high and the rip fence ¾" from the opposite side of the teeth. Use the thickness of one of the pyramid layers to set the rip fence. With the back of the stair stack down against the table, and one end of the stack against the rip fence, use the miter gauge to push the stack past the blade. Lower the blade to 13⁄16" high and move the rip fence to 2¼" from the far side of the teeth. Saw through the stack again, with its back against the fence and its bottom on the table. This second cut is shown in photo 1.

6 The stairs fit into notches in the layers, and should slide into them nicely. Layer 1 (B) has a shallow notch, so we'll begin there. Set the blade of the table saw 9⁄16" high. Set the rip fence slightly more than 3¼" from the near side of the teeth. We'll sneak up on a good fit. With a layer blank held upright against the miter gauge and one of its edges against the rip fence, push the square past the blade. Then rotate the square so that the opposite edge is against the rip fence, and make another cut, as shown in photo 2. The stairs shouldn't fit between these kerfs yet. Cut out some of the waste on the band saw to make testing the fit easier. Move the rip fence gradually closer to the blade, cutting both sides of the notch after each adjustment, until you have a good fit around the stairs.

7 Once the rip fence is properly adjusted, raise the blade to 2⅞" high. Make shoulder cuts with this setting in the remaining eight squares.

8 On layer 1, draw a line ½" from the front edge across the notch area. Saw to this line on the band saw, cutting from one side and then the other until all the waste is removed.

9 Draw a 4" square in the center of one of the other squares. Beginning in one of the shoulder cuts, use the band saw to remove the inside of this 4"-square area, right up to the lines, as shown in photo 3. Now you have two options for removing squares of the same dimensions from the remaining seven layers. You can draw the 4" square on each and saw out the waste accurately, as you just did. A faster and more accurate method involves pattern-routing the waste with a flush-trimming router bit, as described in the following steps.

PHOTO 4

10 Trace the square in the pattern piece onto the other seven layers. Saw out as much of the 4" square as you dare from each of them, but don't saw outside the lines. That would defeat the purpose of the flush trimmer, wouldn't it?

11 Put a ball-bearing flush-trimming cutter in your router, and mount your router in a router table. Set the depth-of-cut so that the ball bearing rides in the middle of the pattern piece, about 1⅛" above the table. Mark the top faces of all the squares, so that they are sure to line up later. Put two pieces of double-sided tape on a face of one of the seven squares. Press the neatly sawn square (the pattern) on top, aligning the edges exactly. Rout out the waste, pushing against the rotation of the cutter and keeping your fingers on the outside edges of the blanks (see photo 4). Repeat this procedure with the other six squares.

12 Now we'll bevel each pyramid layer and cut it to finished size. Tilt the table-saw blade to 10°. Set the rip fence on the "open" side of the blade to barely bevel the edge of layer 1 (the square with the small notch and no 4" hole). With layer 1 face down, bevel all four edges (see photo 5).

PHOTO 5

13 Reserve the pattern square for layer 9 (J), the smallest layer, because its square corners will fit the inside walls of the temple nicely. Move the rip fence ¼" closer to the blade and bevel two adjoining edges of the next square, again cutting with its top face down. Again move the rip fence ¼" closer and cut the two remaining edges of layer 2 (C). Stack layer 2 on layer 1 to check your work. Throughout the bevelling process, keep the layers stacked in order. This will help you keep track of your progress. Photo 6 shows my stacks a little over halfway through the bevelling job. No, I didn't leave them on the table saw while I was cutting. One more word about safety: Be sure to hold both arms of the squares as they go past the saw blade, so that they cut evenly, without deflecting.

14 Without moving the rip fence, bevel two adjoining edges of layer 3. (At this point, layer 3 should be 9" square.) Move the rip fence ¼" closer, and bevel two adjoining edges of layer 4. Repeat this process of moving the rip fence ¼" and cutting only two edges for each of the remaining layers.

15 Now we'll go back to layer 3 and bevel its other two edges. Use layer 2 to return the rip fence to the last setting you used to cut it. From there, move the rip fence ½" closer to the blade, and bevel the two remaining edges of layer 3. Keep moving the rip fence ½" closer to bevel each succeeding layer.

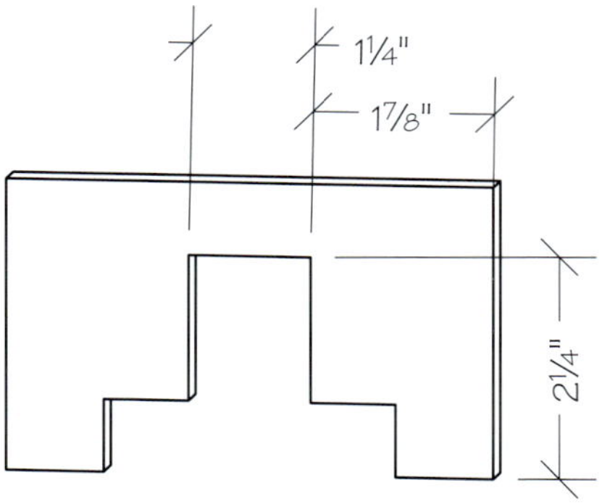

FIGURE 3. **Front Opening**

PHOTO 6

ASSEMBLING THE PYRAMID AND MAKING THE TEMPLE

1 Apply glue to the notched area of the stairs, and hold the stairs in place on layer 1. Position layer 2 on top of layer 1 to check the placement of the stairs. Then drill two #6 pilot holes through layer 1 and into the stairs. Drive 1⅝" screws to anchor the stairs.

2 Drill #6 pilot holes, well countersunk, through layer 2 and into layer 1, in the corners of the layers. Apply glue to the bottom of layer 2, and replace it on layer 1. Drive 1¼" screws to fasten the layers.

3 Repeat step 2 to add layers 3–8 to the pyramid.

4 Cut the front and back (K), sides (L), and roof (M) to size on the table saw.

5 Use the information in figure 3 to draw the door opening on the front. Put layer 9 in place, hold the front centered against the back of the stairs, and trace the stairs onto the front. Cut out the waste on the bandsaw or with a jigsaw. Pare the notch for the stairs with a sharp chisel until the notch just fits the stairs.

6 Glue the front and back to the edges of the sides, clamp them, and put them on top of layer 9, aligning the temple with the stairs and the square opening, as shown in photo 7. When the glue has cured, drill two angled 1⁄16" pilot holes through each joint. Drive 4d finishing nails, and set the nail heads. Putty those holes now, if you wish—there won't be any more nails.

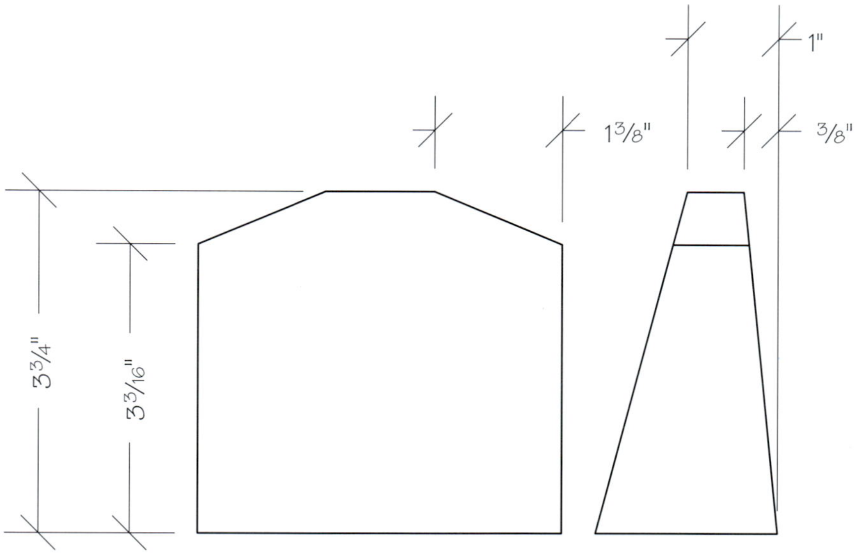

FIGURE 4. **Crown Front and Side Views**

7 Apply glue to the bottom edges of the temple, and hold it in place on layer 9 for a few minutes. Remove the temple and layer 9 together, carefully, and turn them over. Drill three #6 pilot holes, one per side and one in back, and countersink them, as shown in photo 8. Drive 1⅝" screws in the holes.

8 Put the roof on the temple walls, aligning all edges, and drill pilot holes for #6 screws, two into the front and two into the back. Countersink enough to let the screw heads sink slightly below the surface, and drive 1¼" screws. The roof will remain removable for yearly temple purification rites.

PHOTO 7

PHOTO 8

AMERICA'S FIRST SKYSCRAPERS

IN NORTHERN GUATEMALA, AT THE BASE OF THE YUCATAN Peninsula, lie the ruins of a major Mayan center called Tikal. Its pyramids, temples, and ceremonial buildings mark a site inhabited from perhaps 600 B.C. until the tenth century, when it was abandoned. At the height of its power and architectural accomplishment, from A.D. 600 to A.D. 800, about 10,000 people lived within its six square miles, and the city drew on a neighboring population of 60,000. Sitting in a low-lying rain forest—so low that residents built their huts on mounds to keep them dry in rainy weather—the five principal temples in the Tikal complex soar above the surrounding trees. At 148 feet, the fourth tallest of the Tikal pyramids, Tikal I supports the Temple of the Jaguar and contained the tomb of a Mayan king, Ah Cacao.

The pyramids at Tikal were built with cores of stone rubble and concrete faced with thin limestone slabs. They have small rooms in their temples, limited in size by their corbel vaults. In corbel construction, horizontal members, or *corbels*, are embedded deeply enough in a wall to ensure that their exposed portions can support weight. The ceiling of a corbel vault therefore looks like an inverted stairway. Such construction indicates that the Mayans did not know about curved arches. The rooms were finished in white stucco.

Architectural historian Vincent Sculley suggests that the Tikal pyramids embody the human image in an architectural form. Tikal I's height, regal bearing, and its high crown certainly support the notion that it represents Ah Cacao to the ages. Its steep stairway, though eased from the precipitous pyramid walls, enforces awe with its difficulty of approach. Furthermore, Ah Cacao's queen, Lady Twelve Macaw, Tikal II, sits across the plaza. True to the image carved into the lintel of her temple, her pyramid is short and broad, more approachable than her husband's, and has a wide top that easily accommodates her temple. While little is known about the Tikal Mayans or how they used their ceremonial buildings, Ah Cacao clearly understood how to impress his subjects.

PHOTO BY GAYLN C. HAMMOND, HAMMOND PHOTOGRAPHY, MONTEREY, CA

PHOTO 9

9 Apply glue to the bottom of layer 9, center it on top of layer 8, and clamp from the bottom of the pyramid to the roof. Make sure that the clamps don't move the glue joint (see photo 9).

10 Cut three 4" squares from ¾" plywood, and glue them into a stack for the crown (N).

11 When the glue has dried, trim one edge flat for the bottom of the crown. Use the information in figure 4 to draw the profile of the crown on one side edge. Cut to these lines on the band saw, as shown in photo 10. Save the fatter of the offcut wedges, and tape it back in place to provide a firm footing for the next step.

PHOTO 10

PHOTO 11

12 Draw its top outline on the sawn face of the crown, and remove the waste on the band saw (see photo 11).

13 Position the crown on the roof, centering it widthwise and 1" from the back. Trace the crown onto the roof. Apply glue to the bottom of the crown, and hold it firmly in place on the roof until the glue begins to set. When the glue has dried, remove the roof/crown assembly from the temple, and drill two countersunk pilot holes for #6 screws through the roof and into the crown. Fasten the crown to the roof with 1⅝" screws.

PAINTING THE PYRAMID

1 Prime the entire pyramid. When the primer has dried, sand all surfaces except the front of the stairs, using 150-grit sandpaper.

2 This birdhouse lends itself well to spray painting. Choose a color that approximates limestone, and be sure to spray outdoors on a warm day.

JAPANESE PAGODA
SAPSUCKER HOUSE

ARCHITECT: Unknown

Does that spire look impossibly thin? Do those roofs and ribs look too hard to make? Don't worry: you don't have to be a Buddhist—or even an expert woodworker—to make this charming birdhouse. Go carefully on your way, one step at a time, listening to the master, and you'll be fine.

MATERIALS

3/8" exterior plywood, 1/4 sheet
1/2" exterior plywood, 1/4 sheet
Pine, 1 x 4 x 6'

SUPPLIES

3d finishing nails
#6 x 1 1/4" decking screws
1/16" drill bit and 1 1/2" Forstner bit
#6 pilot bit

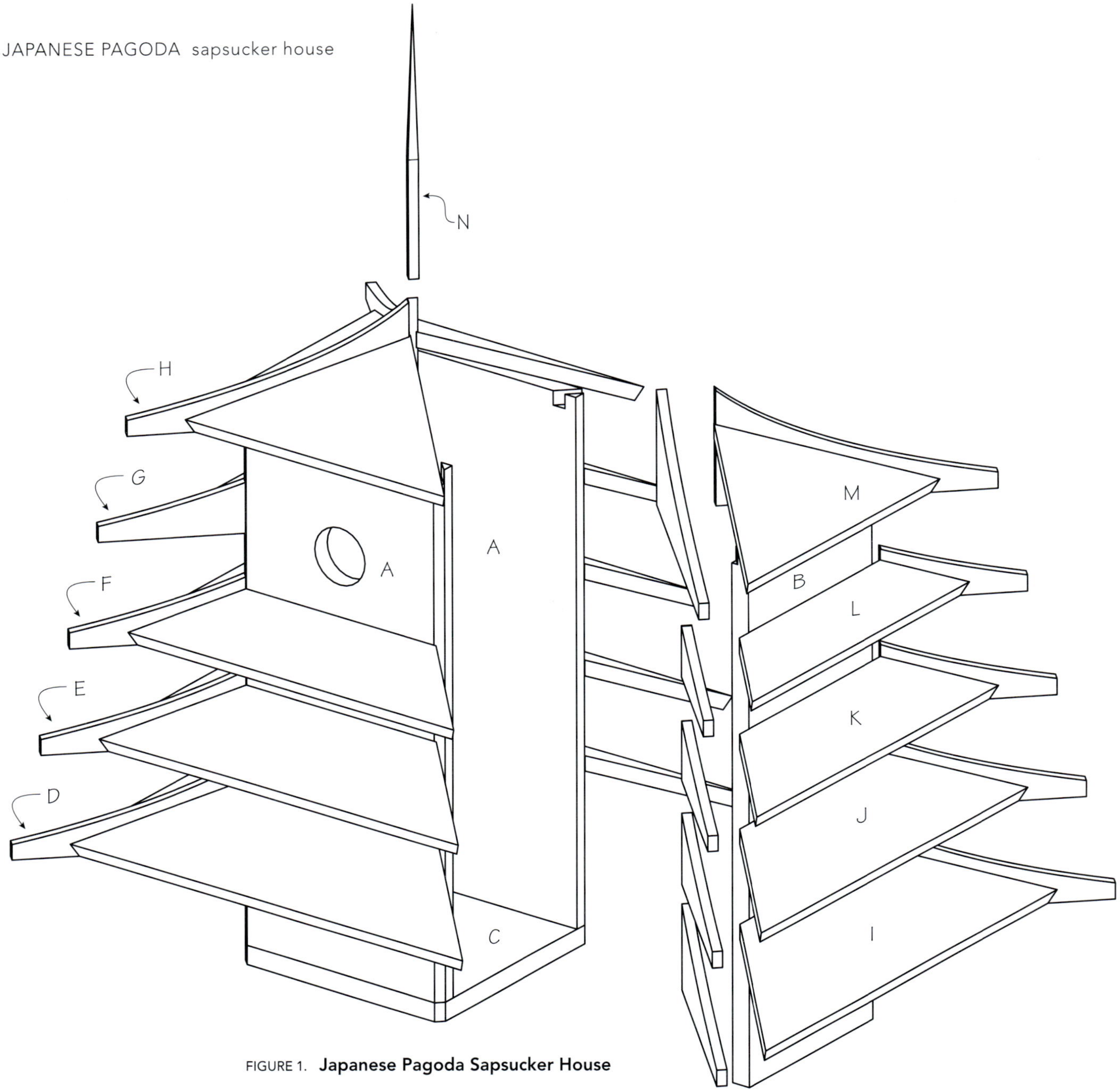

FIGURE 1. **Japanese Pagoda Sapsucker House**

CUTTING LIST

CODE	DESCRIPTION	QTY.	MATERIAL	DIMENSIONS
A	Front/back	2	plywood	1/2" x 6" x 14"
B	Sides	2	plywood	1/2" x 5" x 14"
C	Floor	1	plywood	1/2" x 6" x 6"
D	Bottom ribs	4	plywood	1/4" x 2 1/4" x 5 5/8"
E	Second ribs	4	plywood	1/4" x 1 7/8" x 5"
F	Third ribs	4	plywood	1/4" x 1 5/8" x 4 1/4"
G	Fourth ribs	4	plywood	1/4" x 1 3/8" x 3 1/2"
H	Top ribs	4	plywood	1/4" x 3" x 6 7/8"
I	Bottom roofs	4	plywood	3/8" x 3 1/2" x 11 3/4"
J	Second roofs	4	plywood	3/8" x 3" x 10 3/4"
K	Third roofs	4	plywood	3/8" x 2 3/8" x 9 3/4"
L	Fourth roofs	3	plywood	3/8" x 1 3/4" x 8 3/4"
M	Top roofs	4	plywood	3/8" x 4 3/8" x 7 3/4"
N	Spire	1	pine	1/4" x 1/4" x 7"

MAKING THE NESTING BOX

1 All outside faces of the assembled nesting box, consisting of the front, back, and sides, must be exactly the same width. This will make cutting the roofs easier later on. Measure two thicknesses of your plywood, stacked together, and adjust the width of the sides (B) to achieve a perfectly square construction. Cut out the front/back (A), sides (B), and floor (C).

2 With the table-saw blade tilted to 45°, cut a ¼"-wide bevel on the two outside corners of the front/back pieces, as shown in photo 1. Refer to figure 2 to mark the center of the entrance hole on the front, and bore a 1½" hole.

3 Draw lines square across the front, back, and sides at the positions shown in figure 2. These indicate the top edges of the roofs.

4 Glue one edge of a side, and clamp it flush with an edge of the front. Make sure that the joint is square, as shown in photo 2. (To bring the joint to square, adjust the angles of the clamps. A small change in the position of the clamp pads—or even the amount of pressure—can make a big difference.) As soon as you're sure that the glue is sticking, add the other side to the front in the same way. Then glue the back to the sides. Drill four 1⁄16" angled pilot holes through each joint, and reinforce the joints with 3d finishing nails. Drill the holes away from the bevel so that the nail heads don't change the shape of the bevel when you set them. Set the nail heads, and putty the holes. Sand the putty flush using 150-grit sandpaper.

5 Position the floor on the bottom end of the box. Drill one countersunk pilot hole for #6 screws through the floor and into each of the four bottom edges. Drive 1¼" screws, but don't glue the floor in place. You'll want to remove it for yearly housecleaning.

6 Use a low-angle block plane or a bastard file to bevel the corners of the floor to match the bevels on the front and back of the house.

7 To mark the notches for the top ribs (H), hold a piece of ¼" pine, on edge, diagonally across the top of the house. Trace the pine with a sharp pencil on top of each corner. These lines should end at the corners of the bevels on the front and back pieces.

8 Use a fine-toothed saw, such as a dozuki, to cut just inside the lines to a depth of ½", as shown in photo 3. Pare out the waste with a sharp chisel.

PHOTO 2

PHOTO 3

PHOTO 1

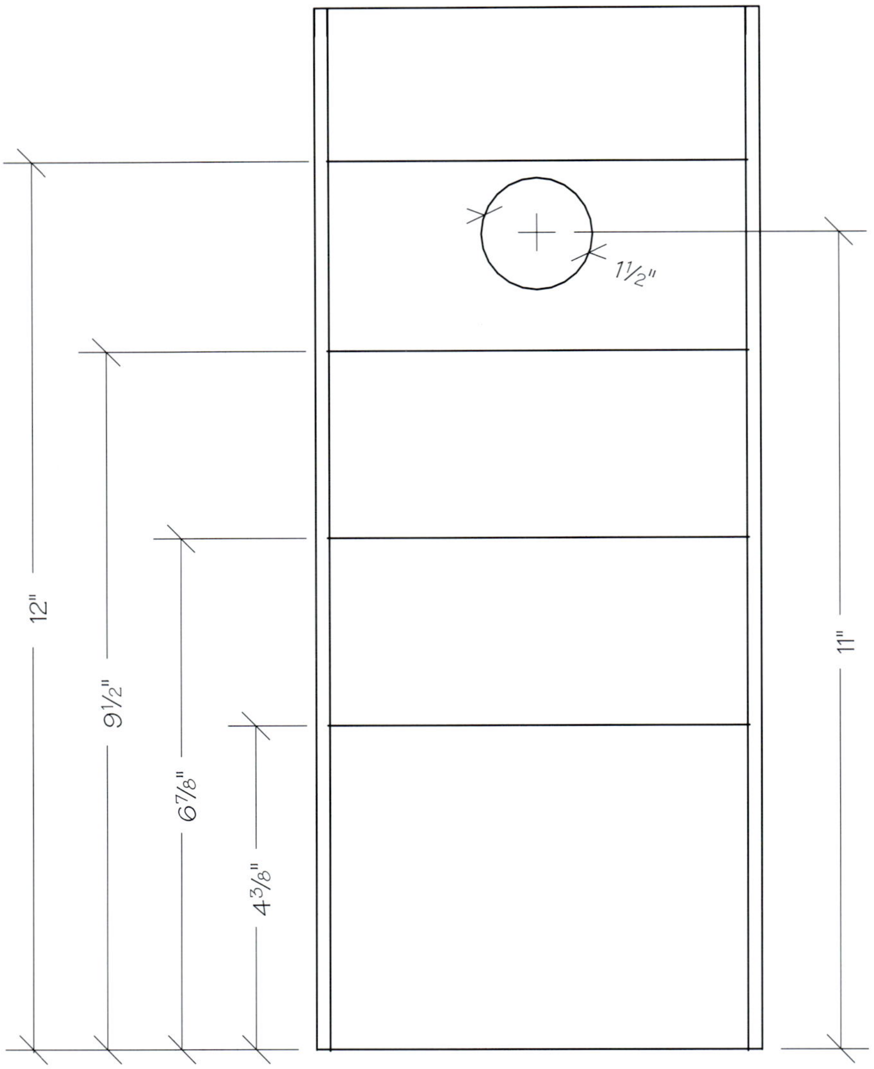

FIGURE 2. **Front**

PHOTO 4

PHOTO 5

MAKING THE RIBS AND ROOFS

1 As figure 3 shows, all the ribs (D–H) have the same profile, and you can make the lower ones by cutting the inside ends from top ribs (H). So that's what we'll do. Begin by cutting 20 rib blanks into 3 x 6⅞" rectangles. Make a pattern for the top ribs from figure 3, and trace the pattern onto five of the rectangles.

2 Make five stacks of rectangles, with a traced piece on top. Use masking tape to keep the stacks aligned as you saw out the rib profile on the band saw. Sand the curves smooth using 100- and 150-grit sandpaper.

3 Cut all but the top ribs to length.

4 To make gluing the roofs to the house easier, make eight 25° wedges from scrap plywood. You can do this easily on a table saw by alternately cutting across a piece of scrap plywood at 25° and 0°, as shown in photo 4. Measuring from the sharp angle, cut two wedges to 1¼", two to 1¾", two to 2¼", and two to 2¾".

5 Cutting the roofs (I–M) is a little tricky, but the following procedure will help you achieve good results. All of the inside edges of the four lower roofs (I–L) have 25° bevels, so begin by bevelling strips from which to cut the roofs. For each roof size, saw out a strip to width—long enough for all the roofs of that size—with one square edge and one bevelled edge.

6 Return the table-saw blade to perpendicular, and rip enough plywood 4⅜" wide for the top roofs (M).

7 Prepare a stop block for cutting the roofs. It should have a 42° angle on one end and be a convenient size for clamping to your miter gauge (see photo 5).

8 The inside (bevelled) edges of all the lower roofs are the same length (the width of the faces of the house box); however, their ends must be cut at compound angles. Tilt the blade of your table saw to 17.5°. With the miter gauge on the open (obtuse angle) side of the blade, and its farther end forward, set its angle to 42°. Use a protractor and a bevel gauge to set the saw accurately. With its bevelled edge forward and down, cut the right end of every roof piece, as shown in photo 6. Be sure to leave enough length for each roof size.

9 Now set the miter gauge to 42° in the opposite direction, so that its outer end is nearest you. With its bevelled edge against the miter gauge, cut the other end of one roof piece, but leave it longer than its final dimension (see photo 7). Use that end and any of the other roof pieces to check your miter gauge angle, by holding them end-to-end against two adjacent sides of the nesting box. Adjust the miter gauge as necessary, and test the angle again. While you're there, mark a roof piece to the accurate distance between the bevels on the box.

10 Set the stop block to cut a roof slightly oversize. Use that roof and two rib pieces to check its length. Adjust the stop block, and keep checking the length until you have a perfect fit. Then cut all the bevelled roofs to length.

11 While your saw is properly adjusted (but without the stop block), cut the left side of each top roof.

PHOTO 6

PHOTO 7

12 Reverse the angle of the miter gauge to 42°, as it was set for the first cut on the lower roofs. Cut the right side of each top roof, forming a sharp corner at the top of the roof.

FIGURE 3. **Rib Patterns**

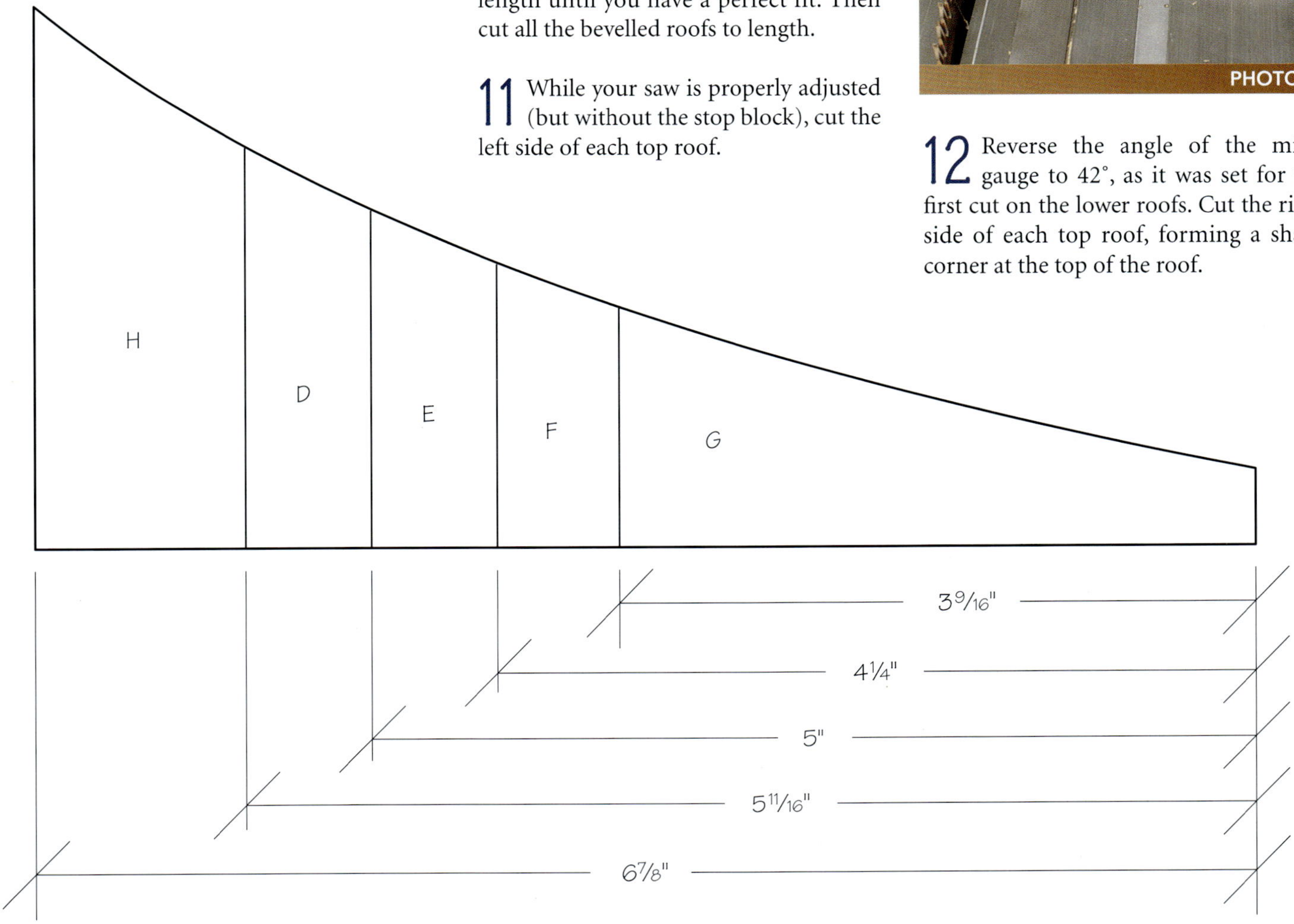

PHOTO 8

PHOTO 9

PHOTO 10

PHOTO 11

ASSEMBLING THE ROOFS AND RIBS

1 Gluing the roofs and the ribs to the box takes patience, but, as you know already, a pagoda isn't built in a day. We'll glue the roofs to one side of the box first, then work our way around the box, adding all the ribs and the roofs before moving to an adjacent side. The fact that the bottom outside edge of the roofs is even with the bottom edge of the ribs makes this process somewhat easier. Lay the box, entrance hole down, on your bench, and sort out all the ribs and roofs. Find the 25° wedges you made long ago. Apply glue to the bevelled edge of a bottom roof, and hold it firmly against the box, aligning its top edge even with the line and its ends even with the bevels. Hold two of the wedges against the bottom of the roof to help maintain its angle. When the glue begins to hold, add the second, third, and fourth roofs in the same way, as shown in photo 8.

2 From three pieces of scrap plywood, make a simple U-shaped support at least 4½" high so that the roofs and ribs won't hit your bench as you work on the other sides of the pagoda. You can see the support at the bottom of photo 9.

3 Put the pagoda on its new support, with one of the sides up. Apply glue to the uppermost end of the bottom roof and to the inside end of a bottom rib, and press the rib in place, with its bottom edge even with the bottom corner of the bottom roof. (That's a lot of bottoms, but the point is that they should be even.) Apply glue to an end and a bevelled edge of another bottom roof, and hold it in position against the rib and even with the horizontal line on the box. Add a rib and a roof at the other levels on this side, as shown in photo 9.

4 When the glue has set sufficiently, turn the pagoda to the opposite side, and add another rib and another roof at each level.

5 When you're ready for the front roofs, glue the remaining ribs in place first. When the glue holds them securely, check the length of each roof (except the fourth, of course) by holding it in place. If a roof doesn't fit just right, as is likely, don't fret—I'll tell you how to fix it. You can effectively lengthen a roof by removing a little of its bevelled edge. So, if a roof is too short, plane its bevelled edge until the roof fits. If the roof is too long, you must cut a little from one end. Or had you figured that part out already? Fit the three front roofs, and glue them in place.

6 It's time to make the last piece of the pagoda—the spire (N). Its thicknesses should match that of the ribs. You can leave the spire square or taper it as shown, but leave the bottom 3" square.

7 Glue the inside edges of two top ribs to the spire, as shown in photo 10, keeping the assembly flat on the bench and making sure that the bottom edges form a straight line. Hold the pieces tight until the glue begins to cure.

8 Add the two remaining ribs, as shown in photo 11, in which I'm using the square corners of two pieces of scrap plywood to keep the angles true.

ORIGINS OF JAPANESE DESIGN

IN ALL CULTURES, RELIGION HAS BEEN THE ORIGINAL DRIVING force of architecture. Japan got off to a slow start in this regard, since its indigenous religion, Shinto, derived from nature worship, and required no images. Buildings weren't needed to house religious paraphernalia, nor to protect worshipers from the (natural) elements. Eventually, shrines were erected as visiting sites for gods, but even these did not lead to any monumental architecture, because they needed to be destroyed and rebuilt during periodic purification rites. These shrines had no foundations; in fact, Japanese architectural practice was limited to post-and-beam construction with thatched roofs.

Beginning in 552, the Japanese aristocracy accepted Buddhism, which was introduced from Korea in that year. The religion brought with it Chinese-style Buddhist temples, which must have impressed the Japanese with their graceful eaves, tile roofs, ornate brackets, bright paint, and their crowning spires. In addition, impressively designed compounds surrounded the temples, incorporating covered corridors and imposing walls. All this was so new and so attractive to the aristocrats that they imported Chinese architects and artisans, who built 46 temples in Japan by 625. Within the next 100 years, native architects began to change the Chinese pattern, making their temples more Japanese. These early changes included adding more pagodas to the temple compounds and adding covered balconies to pagodas, doubling the apparent number of stories and emphasizing their horizontal lines.

At the beginning of the ninth century, two new Buddhist sects, the Tendai and Shingon, were introduced to Japan. Ironically, these imports spurred the development of an indigenous Japanese architectural style. Because the new sects favored mountaintop locations for their temples, the symmetrical plans of the relatively flat, lowland compounds had to be abandoned. This encouraged a native proclivity for asymmetry and careful juxtapositions. As Japan became isolated from China in the tenth century, more indigenous materials were used in temples, such as cypress-bark roofs instead of tile, and wooden floors instead of stone. The abstraction and the use of organic materials associated with Japanese design are rooted in the adaptation of early temple architecture.

PHOTO BY GALYN C. HAMMOND, HAMMOND PHOTOGRAPHY, MONTEREY, CA

PHOTO 12

PHOTO 13

9 Add another plywood scrap to your setup, and clamp the plywood around the ribs, as shown in photo 12, for support while you're gluing the first top roof. Find the angle at which the roof meets both ribs, and mark the ribs. Apply glue to the edges of the roof, and push it back in place, holding it firmly until the glue holds.

10 Remove one of the pieces of plywood, then fit and glue the next roof. Add the other two roof pieces in the same way, as shown in photo 13. Let the glue cure at least for a couple of hours.

11 Make sure that the top ribs fit into the slots in the walls, and that the slots are deep enough to allow the top roofs to touch the top corners of the walls. Run a line of glue along the outside corners at the tops of the walls, and put a little glue in the slots. Push the top roof assembly into place. Drill two 1/16" pilot holes per side, through the top roofs and into the top edges of the box. Try to hit the outside corner of the box sides with your bit. Carefully drive 3d finishing nails, and set their heads. Putty the holes.

PAINTING THE PAGODA

1 Remove the floor to keep from painting it tight. Prime all exposed plywood edges. When the primer has dried, sand the edges with 150-grit sandpaper, and prime the pagoda. Sand it again.

2 I tried to produce a rough interpretation of the colors of a traditional pagoda, but this design is so spirited that it lends itself to wacky combinations. There's a lot of cutting-in with a paintbrush, but the results are worth the trouble.

OCTAGON HOUSE BIRDFEEDER

ARCHITECT: Vernacular

Octagon houses were supposed to provide a spiritually uplifting living space, but the most we can expect from this one is material sustenance. This feeder will hold a lot of sunflower seeds and provide a dining room for many birds. While they add to the labor involved, the windows allow you to monitor the seed level. This project requires some operations, such as bevelling and pattern routing, that may be new to you, but the construction is quite straightforward. As you can see, it produces a classic birdfeeder.

CUTTING LIST

CODE	DESCRIPTION	QTY.	MATERIAL	DIMENSIONS
A	Canopies	8	plywood	3/4" x 2" x 5 3/4"
B	Walls	8	plywood	3/4" x 4 1/8" x 13"
C	Spacers	16	basswood or pine	1/4" x 1/2" x 3/8"
D	Lower windows	8	glass	3/32" x 2 7/16" x 4 13/16"
E	Upper windows	8	glass	3/32" x 2 7/16" x 4 3/16"
F	Base	1	plywood	3/4" x 14" x 14"
G	Fences	8	hardwood	1/4" x 1 1/8" x 6"
H	Roofs	8	plywood	1/2" x 5" x 6 7/8"
I	Roof support	1	plywood	3/4" x 7 1/2" x 7 1/2"

FIGURE 1.
Octagon House Bird Feeder

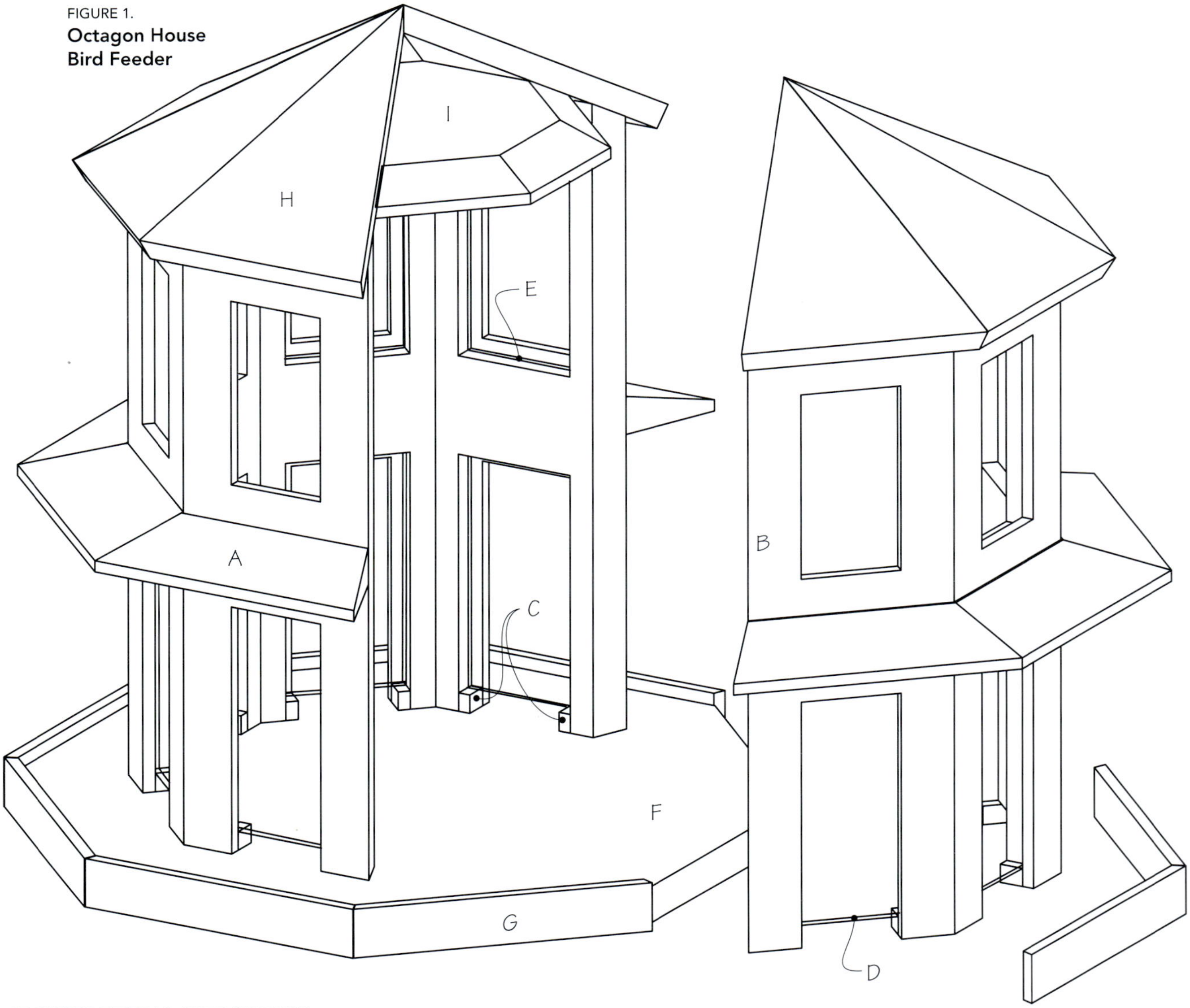

PHOTO 1

PHOTO 2

PHOTO 3

MATERIALS
- 1/2" exterior plywood, 1/8 sheet
- 3/4" exterior plywood, 1/4 sheet
- Double-strength glass, 12" x 18"
- Basswood or pine, from scrap
- Mahogany or oak, from scrap

SUPPLIES
- 3d finishing nails
- #6 x 1" decking screws
- #6 x 1 5/8" decking screws
- 1/16", 1/4", 5/16", and 1/2" drill bits
- #6 pilot bit
- #0 biscuits
- Double-sided (carpet) tape
- Glazier's points
- Glazing putty
- 1/4" x 2' to 3' threaded rod, washers, and nuts

MAKING THE WALLS

1 To prepare stock for the canopies, cut a strip of ¾" plywood measuring 2" x 48". Tilt the blade on your table saw to 15°, and set the rip fence on the "open" side of the blade to barely bevel the 2" width of the strip. Finish the cut by pushing your canopy blank with some scrap until the blank clears the blade. (See photo 1.) Sand the bevelled face and the narrow edge.

2 Use the stop on your miter gauge to cut eight 5⅞" canopy (A) pieces from the strip. We'll glue these to the walls before trimming them to their finished sizes.

3 Saw eight pieces for the walls (B) from ¾" plywood, cutting them oversize in width to 5⅞", then crosscutting each piece 13" long. Using the stop on the miter gauge, and the table-saw blade tilted to 30°, cut a bevel on one end of each piece (see photo 2). On the shorter, outside face of each piece, square a line across, 6" from the unbevelled, or bottom end of the wall.

4 On the outside face of one of the wall pieces, draw two rectangles for the windows, as detailed in figure 2. Cut to the lines of the open rectangle on the band saw or with a jigsaw. Drill a ½" hole inside each of the corners of the closed rectangle, and saw to the lines with a jigsaw. Clean up the saw marks, and straighten the sides, using a sharp chisel, a bastard file, or 100-grit sandpaper on a block.

5 You can cut the window openings in the other seven walls in the same way if you wish. Alternatively, to finish quicker and more accurately, you can use a ball-bearing flush-trimming router bit guided by the first wall. Trace the window openings onto each of the other walls, and cut out as much of the waste as you dare with the drill bit and jigsaw. Put a strip of double-sided tape on the second wall, and press the first wall onto it, matching all edges precisely. With the router mounted in its table, rout the waste from both rectangles, as shown in photo 3. Remember to move the work against the rotation of the cutter for better control. And never put your fingers inside the rectangle you're cutting. Repeat for the other six walls. Square the corners with a bastard file, working from the outside faces.

6 Put a piloted, ¼" rabbeting bit in the router table, and set it to cut ½" high. Cut rabbets around both openings on the back of each wall. To make the cutting easier on you and your router, you may wish to take two ¼"-deep cuts to reach the ½" depth. Square the corners with a sharp chisel.

7 Cut the spacers (C), and glue them into the rabbets at the bottom of each wall. These little blocks will keep the glass ⅜" above the base (F).

8 Apply glue to the back edge of a canopy, and press it into place, with its unbevelled side at the 6" line (from step 3) on the outside of a wall. Try to match the ends of the canopy with the edges of the wall. Hold the canopy firmly for a few minutes to allow the glue to stick. Repeat with the other canopies and walls.

9 Drill two pilot holes for #6 screws through each wall and into each canopy, at least 1½" inside the edges. Make sure to cut enough countersink to bury the screw heads. Angle the pilot holes toward the narrow edge of the canopy because you'll be driving 1⅝" screws. So go ahead and drive the screws, already.

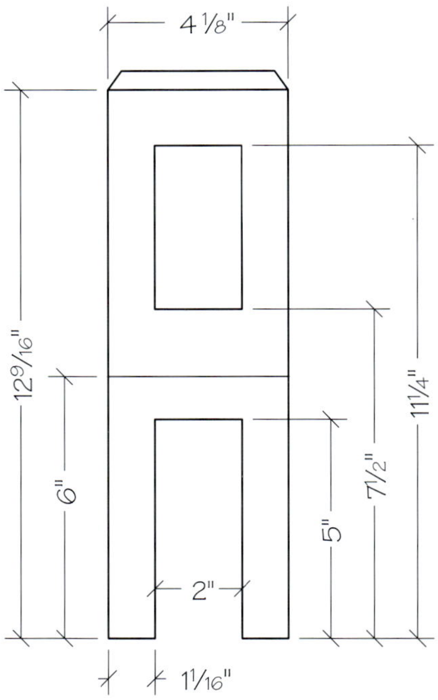

FIGURE 2. **Wall**

CUTTING BEVELS AND ASSEMBLING THE WALLS

1 Tilt the table-saw blade to 22½°, and set the rip fence 4 11/16" from the blade, measured at the table. Check that the blade is raised higher than 2¾" to cut completely through the wall assemblies and their canopies. Make sure that the canopy doesn't protrude beyond the wall edge that contacts the rip fence. Cut one bevel on each wall. (See photo 4.)

2 Rip a bevelled strip from scrap plywood, at least 1½" wide and 14" long. Use this strip against the rip fence to offset the wall assemblies, then bevel the second side of each wall by moving both pieces past the blade, as shown in photo 5. Set the fence to cut the inside faces of the walls 3 9/16" wide.

3 You can omit this step if you feel very confident that you can glue the walls together without alignment help, but biscuits make the job much easier. Tilt the fence on your biscuit joiner to 22½°, and set it to cut near the inside of a wall edge. At each edge of the outside faces of the walls, mark 2" and 11" from the bottom. Cut slots for #0 biscuits, centering a slot on each of the marks. Photo 6 shows this operation with the biscuit joiner mounted upside down in a vise.

4 Using 150-grit sandpaper, slightly round the outside corners of the window openings. Prime the edges of the window openings, sand them when they're dry, and apply a second coat of primer. Prime the inside faces of the walls, too.

PHOTO 4

PHOTO 5

PHOTO 6

5 When the primer has dried, you can go ahead and glaze the windows (D and E). You could wait until the walls are glued together, but it's much easier to do now. Cut the glass with enough clearance to allow it to drop into the rabbets easily. (For helpful tips, see Simple Glass Cutting on page 12.) Clean the glass. Secure each pane with three or four glazier's points, as shown in photo 7. (You can leave the rabbets open, as I did. For a more finished appearance, use glazing putty, but keep the bevel narrow, just covering the points.) Take a few minutes right now to cover the outside of each window with masking tape. You'll thank me later. Or, rather, you'll kick yourself later if you don't mask now.

6 Find all your spring clamps, tiny C-clamps, clamping pads, and band clamps. Put a little glue in the biscuit slots in the right-hand edge of each wall, pushing in #0 biscuits as you go. From now until the walls are tight together, you must work quickly, without pausing even for a stray thought. Lay out all the walls next to each other on your bench, insides facing up. Run a line of glue on each bevelled edge without biscuits, putting a little in the slots as you go, and apply glue to one edge of each canopy. Pick up two walls and press them snugly together, with the bottom ends even. Keep adding walls until the octagon is closed. Use band clamps to hold the walls together, and apply clamps at the window edges where necessary to close gaps (see photo 8.) Clean up any excess glue.

ADDING THE BASE AND ROOF

1 When the smoke has cleared and the glue has dried, begin the base (F) by cutting a 14" square from ¾" plywood. Stand the wall assembly on the square and center it carefully, so that the four walls are parallel with the sides of the square. Measure out 2" from the other walls (or a distance equal to that between the square and the parallel walls), and draw the diagonal lines. Trace the inside and outside of the wall assembly before you move it, and mark the pieces so that you can put them back together the same way. Cut to the diagonal lines on the table saw or band saw.

2 Drill clearance holes with a #6 pilot bit, drilling through the base near the center of each wall joint between the outlines. Then turn the base over and drill countersinks for screw heads from the bottom of the base. Put the wall assembly upside down on your bench. Lay the base on top, matching your marks from the previous step. Use the clearance holes to guide the #6 pilot bit, and drill into the walls. Fasten the base with #6 x 1⅝" screws.

3 Cut the fences (G) from any hardwood, but not all at once. (Mahogany and oak are both rot-resistant, but these pieces will be painted anyway. We're really using hardwood here to resist bird claws.) Cut the first fence, with 22½° angles at its ends, to fit a particular side of the base. Use a stop on your miter gauge to duplicate the length if you find that your first fence fits other sides as well. Then adjust the stop to cut other lengths to fill the gaps. Glue each fence on after cutting it, holding it flush with the bottom of the base, and using 3d finishing nails in 1/16" pilot holes (see photo 9). Set the nail heads and putty the holes.

PHOTO 7

PHOTO 8

PHOTO 9

PHOTO 10

PHOTO 11

PHOTO 12

PHOTO 13

PHOTO 14

PHOTO 15

4 To make the wedged-shaped roof pieces (H), begin with a piece of ½" plywood, 7" wide and at least 27" long. We'll cut one side (the left side with my saw) of all the wedges first, and then cut the other side. Tilt the table-saw blade to 10°, and rotate the miter gauge 20°, with the end nearer the blade forward. Cut across the plywood, beginning 1" from the foremost corner. Save that first cutoff. Mark the leading edge of the plywood three times at 5½" intervals from the first cut, and cut across at those marks. (See photo 10.) Now you have one (truncated) triangle, three parallelograms, and one trapezoid. Kinda feels like sixth grade, doesn't it? (For extra credit: If you throw away the triangle, where will the two trains meet?)

5 Keeping their good faces up, rotate the parallelograms and the trapezoid 180°. Mark 5½" along the new leading edge of the trapezoid, and cut there to produce a fourth parallelogram. Trim the first three parallelograms, as shown in photo 11, to make their bottom surfaces smaller than their top surfaces.

6 Rotate the miter gauge to the opposite 20° setting. Use the first cutoff against the stop to support each blank, and set the stop to cut a sharp corner at the edge of the blank, as shown in photo 12. Cut one roof segment from the blank; then rotate the remaining portion of the blank to cut a second segment, as shown in photo 13. Repeat those two cuts with the other three blanks to produce six more roof segments.

7 You can use biscuits to help glue the roof together, but the following method works well and produces quick results. Arrange the roof segments with their meeting edges together and their bottom edges even. Two edges will not meet, of course. Tape them tightly together, as shown in photo 14.

8 Gather at least four bar clamps. Flip the roof upside down so that you can apply glue to all the meeting edges. Then turn it right side up again, pull the center upward, and push the two free edges together. Make sure that the top surfaces meet evenly, and apply clamping pressure to the eave edges to hold the roof together while the glue sets. (See photo 15.)

PHOTO BY AL MICHAUD, THE MARKETING WORKS, TRYON, NC

AND IT'S GOOD FOR YOU!

THE OCTAGON HOUSE FORM WAS THE INVENTION OF ORSON Squire Fowler, an American from the rational optimist wing of the wacky, wacky nineteenth century. For thousands of years, octagon buildings had been erected for various purposes, but never for dwellings until Fowler published *A Home for All, or the Gravel Wall and Octagon Mode of Building* (1849). Fowler had his reasons for advocating the octagon: the shape encloses about 25 percent more floor space than a rectangle of the same circumference; it receives more daylight; it's easier to heat and cool; it offers better views; and it requires fewer steps to get from room to room. While none of these arguments withstand rigorous scrutiny—even the increased floor area is partly offset by higher building costs—they sounded good enough to the thousands who built octagons, mostly in the 1860s.

Fowler erected his own octagon in 1850 in Fishkill, New York, using the material he had suggested in his book—concrete. The house incorporated the standard features of the form: two stories with a raised basement, encircling porches, a cupola for extra light and summer cooling, and a minimum of ornamentation. Fowler was also an early adopter of many convenient and hygienic features, such as indoor flush toilets, hot and cold running water, filtered drinking water, speaking tubes, and dumbwaiters.

While Fowler intended octagons to be relatively unadorned forms, the exuberant Victorian impulse to embellish could not restrain itself. Octagon houses were built in every style imaginable, from Gothic to Italianate. This tendency reached its peak at Longwood, a Moorish extravaganza designed by Samuel Sloan for Haller Nutt in Natchez, Mississippi (see photo above). Surrounded by some 8,000 square feet of living space, the four-story central hall ascends to a sixteen-sided belvedere topped by a bulbiform dome containing mirrors to direct sunlight deep into the house. The workmen building "Nutt's Folly," as it was unkindly called, abandoned the job to join the Confederate Army shortly before Haller Nutt died, and Longwood remains unfinished.

9 To lay out the 7½" octagon for the roof support (I), trace the top of the feeder walls on a piece of ¾" plywood, and use your clear plastic ruler (see page 10) to reduce the traced shape to size. Cut out the octagon on the band saw or table saw. Bevel the edges of the roof support by tilting the table-saw blade to 30° and holding one face of the octagon against the rip fence. Move the rip fence as close to the blade as you can, but not so close that the edge of the octagon falls into the blade slot. Cut bevels on each of the eight edges. Photo 16 shows the result.

10 Apply glue to the bevels, and press the roof support into the center of the roof. Drill a pilot hole for a #6 screw about 1" from each edge of the roof support, and drive 1" screws through the support to reinforce the roof, as shown in photo 17.

11 Use a bastard file to flatten a ¾" area at the peak of the roof. Drill a 5⁄16" hole through the peak of the roof and through the center of the roof support. Find the center of the base and drill a ¼" hole through the base. If you intend to mount your feeder on a post, a 17½" length of threaded rod will work to hold the roof in place. Use two washers and two nuts to clamp the rod's bottom end to the base, and another washer and a wing nut above the roof peak. If you want to hang your feeder, the threaded rod must be long enough to allow for filling the feeder—at least 24" and as long as 30". The top wing nut will not be necessary; you can simply slide the roof up the rod to access the inside. Use a coupling to attach a ¼" eye bolt to the top of the rod.

PHOTO 16

PHOTO 17

PAINTING THE FEEDER

1 Sand all unpainted areas of the feeder. Prime the plywood edges twice and everything else once, sanding after each coat. You can spray the finish coats on the walls if you take the time to mask the top surfaces of the canopies. The roof edges and eaves should be the same color as the walls.

2 Once the primary color is dry, remove the masking tape from the windows and the canopies. Then paint the canopies and the roof.

FARNSWORTH HOUSE BIRDFEEDER

ARCHITECT: Mies van der Rohe

This is the original house that people who shouldn't throw stones live in! Even though Philip Johnson's Glass House was completed earlier, he acknowledged that its idea came from Mies. In fact, Mies was a little snippy when he saw Johnson's country house, saying that Johnson didn't "know how to turn a corner." You may think that this feeder holds as much seed as its model offered privacy. Admittedly, not that much! It's a special feeder for special birds, but I'm sure your birds will be grateful for whatever you offer them.

MATERIALS

3/8" exterior plywood, 1/8 sheet
1/2" exterior plywood, 1/8 sheet
Pine, 1 x 4 x 2'
3/8" square aluminum bar, 48"
Double-strength glass, 16" x 20"

SUPPLIES

3d finishing nails
#6 x 1" decking screws
#6 x 1 1/4" decking screws
1/16", 1/8", and 5/32" drill bits
#6 pilot bit
1/4" straight router bit
Metal-working countersink
2 butt hinges, 1" x 2"
Clear silicone caulk

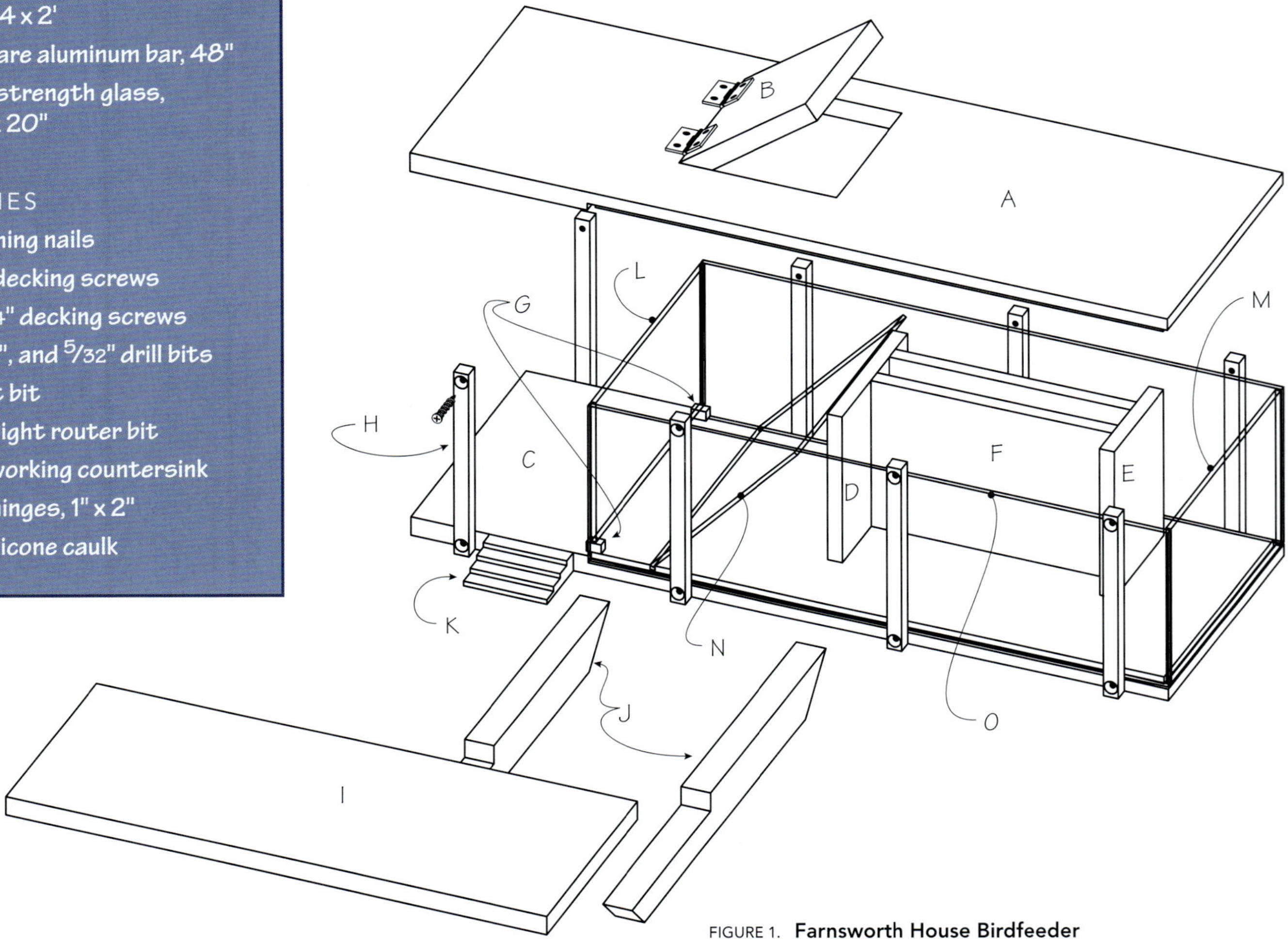

FIGURE 1. **Farnsworth House Birdfeeder**

CUTTING LIST

CODE	DESCRIPTION	QTY.	MATERIAL	DIMENSIONS
A	Roof	1	plywood	1/2" x 7" x 19 1/4"
B	Trap door	1	plywood	1/2" x 4" x 4"
C	Floor	1	plywood	1/2" x 7" x 19 1/4"
D	Wide partition	1	plywood	3/8" x 4" x 4"
E	Narrow partition	1	plywood	3/8" x 3" x 4"
F	Walls	2	plywood	3/8" x 4" x 6 1/8"
G	Glass spacers	2	pine	1/4" x 3/8" x 3/8"
H	Piers*	8	aluminum	3/8" x 3/8" x 5"
I	Deck	1	plywood	1/2" x 5 1/2" x 13 3/4"
J	Deck supports	2	pine	3/4" x 1 1/4" x 11 3/4"
K	Stairs	1	pine	1/2" x 2 1/8" x 1 5/8"
L	Front	1	glass	3/32" x 3 3/4" x 6 5/8"
M	Back	1	glass	3/32" x 4 1/4" x 6 5/8"
N	Ramp	1	glass	3/32" x 5 7/16" x 6 5/8"
O	Sides	2	glass	3/32" x 4 1/4" x 14 3/4"

* Aluminum is easier to work, but you can use mild steel bar stock, which is easier to find.

PHOTO 1

PHOTO 2

PHOTO 3

PHOTO 4

ASSEMBLING THE FRAMEWORK

1 Cut out all the plywood pieces (A–F and I). Note that the roof (A) and the floor (C) must be exactly the same size.

2 Place the trap door (B) on the roof, in the position shown in figure 2 (page 101). Write "top" on the roof so that you can avoid cutting grooves in this surface of the roof. Trace the trap door on the roof using a sharp pencil. Drill ½" holes through the roof, just inside the corners of the square. Use a jigsaw to cut to the pencil lines, as shown in photo 1. Smooth the edges of the hole with a bastard file and 100-grit sandpaper until the trap door slides in place. Put the trap door someplace you'll remember much later.

3 Figure 3 shows the positions of the dadoes and rabbets that will hold the glass walls. The dadoes may be cut using a dado blade and the rip fence on your table saw. Note that the dado in the bottom of the roof is 3/16" deep, while the dado in the floor is ⅛" deep. You can cut the 3/16" x 3/16" rabbets with a ¼" straight router bit, with the help of a long fence clamped to the base of your router. Photo 2 shows the setup I used. Use a sharp chisel to square the rounded ends of the rabbets.

4 Clamp the two walls (F) to a scrap ¾"-thick spacer, and clamp the wide and narrow partitions (D and E) to the ends of the walls, in the positions shown in figure 3. Work with the pieces standing on edge, and make sure the top edges are flush. Loosen the clamp holding the walls to the spacer momentarily to make sure that the partitions lie tight on the ends of the walls. Trace the outsides of the walls on the partitions so you can easily reposition them. Unclamp the partitions, apply glue to the edges of the walls, and clamp the partitions in place again. Drill 1/16" pilot holes through the partitions and into the walls, two per joint at opposing angles. Drive 3d finishing nails into the holes, as shown in photo 3. Wipe off any excess glue.

5 When the glue has dried, position the wall assembly accurately on the floor, as shown in figure 3. Trace the outline of the wall assembly on the floor. Remove the assembly, and drill #6 pilot holes through the floor, one for each wall and partition. Try to center the holes inside your traced lines. Apply glue to the bottom edges of the walls and partitions, and replace the assembly on the floor. Clamp it in place, as shown in photo 4. Turn the package over so that you can extend the pilot holes into the walls and partitions, and drill countersinks for the screw heads. Drive 1¼" screws, then wipe off any excess glue.

PHOTO 5

PHOTO 6

6 Remove the clamp. Position the roof on top of the wall assembly, using a square to make sure that the edges of the roof and the floor are aligned. Follow the procedure in step 5 to drill pilot holes and drive 1¼" screws to hold the roof in place, except that you can't drive a screw in the wide partition. Please don't glue the roof to the wall assembly. The roof must be loose to install the glass.

7 Make the glass supports (G). These provide a ⅜" space for avian access to the sunflower seeds. Glue them to the floor in the positions shown in figure 3, even with the rabbets and extending past the ends of the rabbets by ⅛".

8 Cut the piers (H) to length using a hacksaw or (if they're aluminum) your table saw. Mark both ends of each pier for screw holes, laying out your marks ¼" from each end. Use a center punch and a hammer to make a good starting point for a drill bit. Chuck a 5⁄32" bit in the drill press, and drill clearance holes at each marked point. Use a metal-working countersink in the drill press to allow #6 screw heads to lie flush with the surface of the piers.

9 On the long edges of the roof and floor, mark 17⁄16" and 65⁄16"" from each end. Drill a ⅛" hole at each of those points, using a pier clamped in place to guide the bit, as shown in photo 5. To check your work, temporarily mount all eight piers with two 1¼" screws each. The ends of the piers should be flush with the top and bottom surfaces of the roof and the floor, respectively. Then remove the piers and the roof.

10 Use the information in figure 4 (page 104) to lay out and cut the deck supports (J). Cut the outside shape on the table saw, and then cut the long notch on the band saw or with a jigsaw. Clamp the deck supports to the bottom of the floor, centering them on the front two pier positions, as shown in photo 6. The shoulder of the notch should be flush with the edge of the floor. Drill pilot holes through the floor and into the deck supports, at least 1¼" from each edge of the floor. Countersink enough so that the screw heads will end up below the surface of the floor. Remove the clamps, apply glue to the top edge of each deck support, and fasten the supports to the floor with 1¼" screws.

11 Secure the deck (I) to the deck supports (J) in the same way, but use 1" screws. The deck extends past the inner deck support by 1", the same distance that the floor extends past the other deck support, right? Position the screws 1" and 3½" from the edge of the floor.

12 Cut a piece of pine for the stairs (K). Draw the profile on one side, as shown in figure 4. You can cut the steps by hand, on the band saw, or—very carefully—on the table saw, as I did. If you use the table saw, leave the stair blank long for safety, until the steps are cut. Cut the risers first, using the rip fence. Then cut the steps, beginning with the lowest step, as shown in photo 7. Sand the stairs with 150-grit paper, and glue them in place against the edge of the floor, midway between the first pier and the end of the rabbet.

13 Putty over all nail heads and screw heads. Sand all exposed areas of the house, and round all corners slightly. Find the trap door, and install its hinges and a small screw left proud as a handle. The hinges go on the front side of the trap door. Prime all exposed plywood edges, and sand these surfaces again when the primer has dried. Then prime the whole house and sand it again.

14 Paint the house now, before installing any glass. You can use spray paint, as I did, which is easier if you reinstall the piers and roof. Use a very light grey or beige color—what we used to call, toward the end of a long Minnesota winter, "dark white."

ADDING THE GLASS WALLS

1 If your house has maintained the dimensions given here, you're all set to order your glass. If not, you must adjust the sizes accordingly. To avoid confusion or laughter at the hardware store, be sure to specify "double strength" glass, not "double-thick." (Don't even ask if I speak from experience.) You can cut the glass yourself or have the store cut it for you. Make sure they understand the degree of accuracy you're after: +/– 2 microns. Or tell them "spot on." That makes you sound faintly British and gets their attention. This may not work in all areas of the world. Clean your glass thoroughly.

2 To hold the front (L) and back (M) vertical while you install the sides (O), prepare clamping blocks with one square corner, as shown in photo 8. Remember to pad between the glass and metal, and go easy with the clamping pressure. The glass dimensions allow 1⁄16" clearance between pieces of glass and between the glass and the rabbets. This space will be filled with clear silicone caulk. Cut the nozzle on your caulk tube as close to the end as practical. You'll need small beads of caulk on the edges of the glass to avoid excessive cleanup.

3 Is everyone ready for fun? If you are on good terms with your spouse or significant other, you might want to ask for help with the next few steps. If not, or if either of you is prone to audible, inappropriate blaming, it will be better to soldier on alone. Begin with the ramp (N). Put a continuous bead of caulk on each of its short edges, and lay it in place. The bottom edge hooks into the floor groove, and the top edge leans against the wide partition.

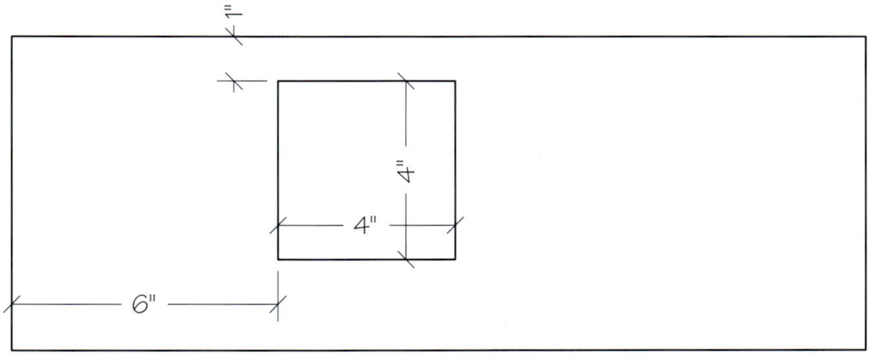

FIGURE 2. **Trap Door Position**

PHOTO BY JON MILLER. © HEDRICH-BLESSING

ALMOST NOTHING

"LESS IS MORE." "GOD IS IN THE DETAILS." THESE ARE THE MOST famous utterances of Mies van der Rohe, and they are not his. His true motto, "almost nothing," better characterizes the spirit of his buildings. This is perhaps nowhere more evident than in the only residence he built in America. Before he emigrated from Germany in 1938, he had become a leading proponent of Modernism, specifically, of the value of stripping away all but the essential. In doing so he had renounced his early buildings with their historical references. After 1921, he employed only abstract geometric forms emphasizing the structure of the building. His 1929 masterwork, the Barcelona Pavilion, epitomized the new style.

When Edith Farnsworth met Mies in 1945, she was aware, as many nonarchitects were not, of his standing in the architectural world. He was also charming and, at 59, quite attractive to women. She was 42, a Chicago physician with a growing academic reputation, and looking for an architect to build a weekend retreat on property she owned on the Fox River. So a bond formed, apparently more professional on his part than on hers. Without that connection, convincing any client to accept a house that was nearly not there might have been difficult, even for Mies.

By the end of 1946, Mies had defined the basic forms of the structure, and his usually deliberate manner of working then concentrated on the interior arrangements. He centralized all of the mechanical elements—plumbing, heating, even roof drainage—within the sole interior structure, which signalled, more than it separated, the different living areas. He also specified the furniture, most of which he had designed for the Tugendhat House (1928–30) in Brno, Czech Republic. Mies supervised construction as well, from the pouring of the concrete roof, floor, and deck slabs to directing the arrangement of the travertine floor panels within the structure's defining grid. Unfortunately, the relationship between architect and client soured, turning into disputes about money which had to be resolved in court. Even though her enthusiasm for the house may have waned with her admiration for Mies, Farnsworth used her retreat for nearly two decades.

PHOTO 8

PHOTO 9

4 Run a continuous bead of caulk into the rabbet around the edge of the floor. There must be enough caulk to keep the glass 1⁄16" from both sides of the rabbet. Put caulk on the short edges of the front, and prop it centered on the spacers. Put caulk on the short edges of the back and press it into place. Don't press downward too much—it should ride at least 1⁄16" above the bottom of the rabbet. The outside of the glass should be flush with the edge of the floor. The house now looks like photo 8, doesn't it?

5 Have the piers and some screws ready. Put the bottom edge of a side (O) into the rabbet, and rotate the top edge toward the pieces of glass already in place. Don't push it into final position yet. Start the screws of two piers into the edge of the floor, and snug the piers against the glass, as shown in photo 9. The piers will hold the glass at a slightly outward angle until you're ready to install the roof. Do the same with the other side.

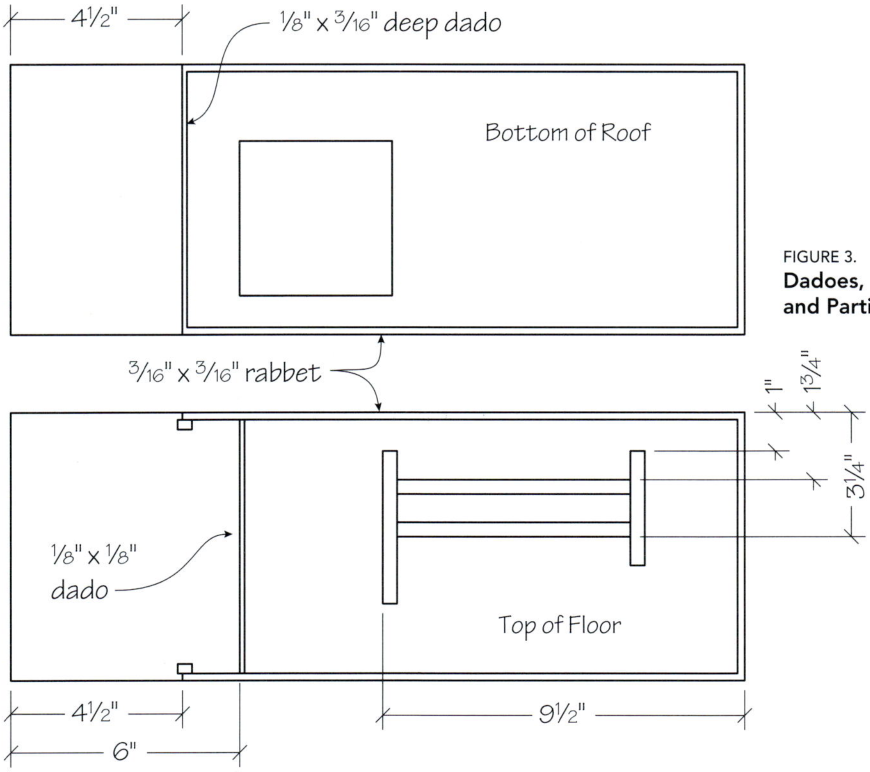

FIGURE 3.
Dadoes, Rabbets, and Partitions

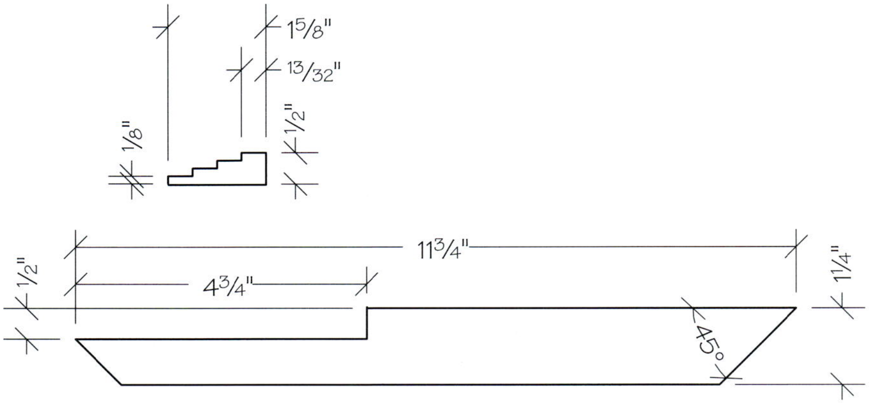

FIGURE 4. **Stairs & Deck Support Profiles**

6 Run a very small bead of caulk into the groove in the roof. Run a continuous bead around the rabbet. Put the three wall/partition screws all the way into their holes. Use the screws to help position the roof, and concentrate on getting the front into its groove first. Hold the back end of the roof above its final position until you're ready to press the sides gradually into place. It would be ideal to push the sides and the top evenly into their final positions. That's impossible, of course, but we must try. Think pure thoughts. Use the wall/partition screws to press the roof downward. Use the top pier screws to help move the sides against the front, ramp, and back. Go slowly to allow the caulk to flow. Don't go so slowly that the caulk starts to harden before all the pieces are happily home.

7 When the caulk has set up, use a single-edge razor blade to clean up excess caulk. Be careful to avoid nicking your lovely paint job.

CHRYSLER BUILDING NUTHATCH HOUSE

ARCHITECT: William van Alen

What bird could resist the chance to live in the most recognizable building of the twentieth century? And this skyscraper has a touching family history. Apparently, one of the reasons Walter P. Chrysler wanted to build a dramatic tower in New York City was to give his sons "something to be responsible for." In order to limit your responsibility, this birdhouse represents only the crowning portion of the Chrysler Building. The project requires many pieces, but you'll need methodical workmanship rather than special woodworking skills to complete it. The finished birdhouse proves that van Alen designed a stunning form, even reproduced in miniature.

CUTTING LIST

CODE	DESC.	QTY.	MATERIAL	DIMENSIONS
A	Arch 1	4	plywood	1/2" x 2" x 11 1/8"
B	Spire	1	pine	1" x 1" x 16"
C	Arch 2	4	plywood	1/2" x 3" x 9 1/4"
D	Arch 3	4	plywood	1/2" x 4" x 7 3/8"
E	Arch 4	4	plywood	1/2" x 5" x 16 1/2"
F	Arch 5	4	plywood	3/8" x 5 3/4" x 17 5/8"
G	Arch 6	4	plywood	3/8" x 6 1/2" x 15 3/4"
H	Arch 7	4	plywood	3/8" x 4 1/2" x 13 7/8"
I	Arch 8	4	plywood	1/4" x 3 3/4" x 13 1/2"
J	Floor	1	plywood	1/2" x 5" x 5"
K	Plinth	4	plywood	1 1/2" x 5" x 6"
L	Screw strip	2	pine	3/4" x 3/4" x 4 3/4"
M	Base	1	plywood	1 1/2" x 7 3/4" x 9"
N	Brace	4	pine	5/8" x 5/8" x 2"

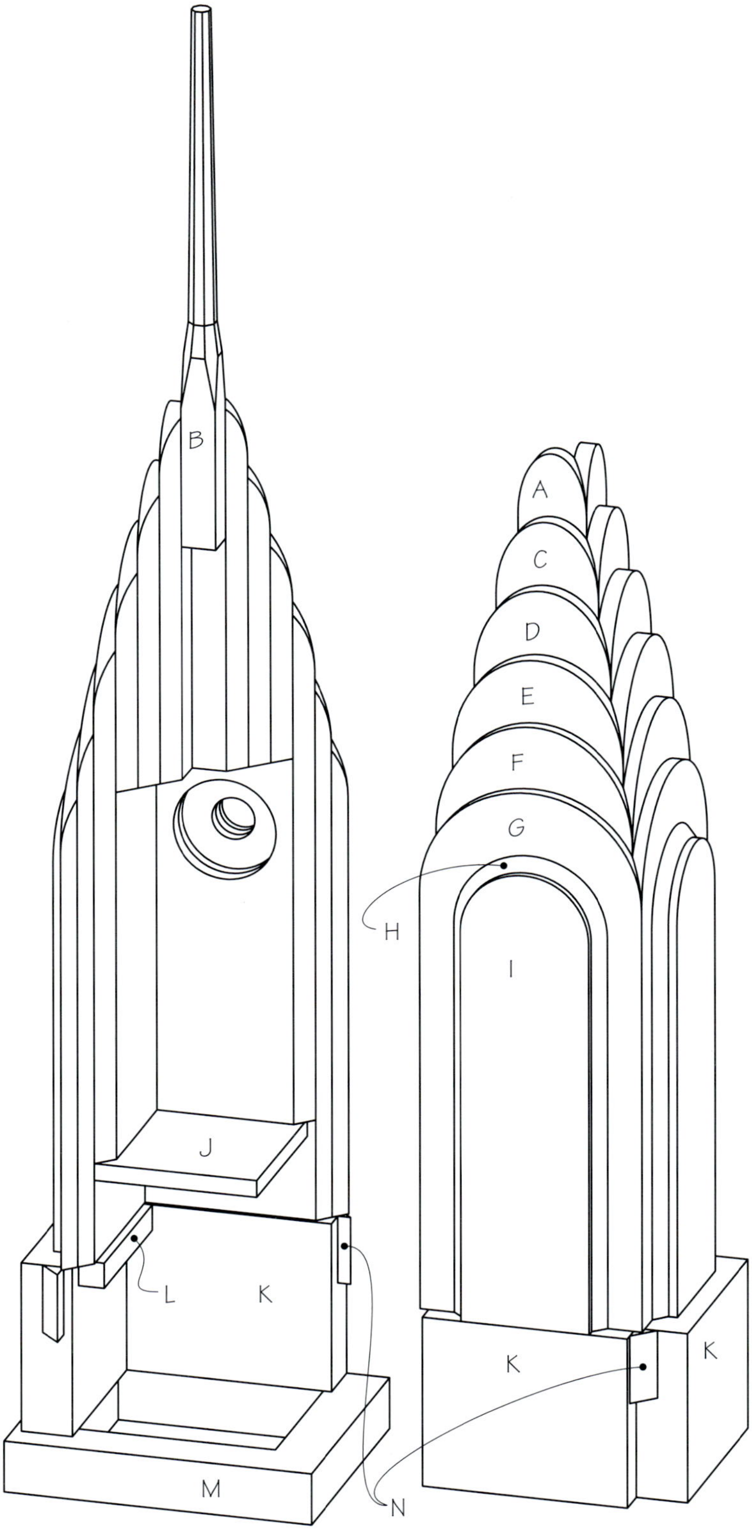

FIGURE 1. **Chrysler Building Nuthatch House**

PHOTO 1

PHOTO 2

PHOTO 3

PHOTO 4

PHOTO 5

NOTE: You can easily change this design to suit bird species that prefer 4" x 4" nesting cavities. The depth of the nesting area can be changed by lengthening or shortening the arch 4 (E) pieces, and you may need to change the size of the entrance hole. Consult the chart on page 136 for specific information.

MATERIALS

¼" exterior plywood, ⅛ sheet
⅜" exterior plywood, ¼ sheet
½" exterior plywood, ¼ sheet
¾" exterior plywood, ⅛ sheet
Pine, from scrap

SUPPLIES

3d finishing nails
#6 x 1⅝" decking screws
#6 x 2" decking screws
#8 x 2½" decking screws
1⁄16" drill bit, 1¼" Forstner bit, and 3" hole saw
#6 and #8 pilot bits

ASSEMBLING THE UPPER ARCHES

1 From the information in figures 2 and 3, make patterns for the eight arches and the spire. Use heavy paper folded in half lengthwise to assure symmetry (see Making Patterns on page 14). By the way, don't throw those patterns away—you can use them again to help paint the windows on the arches.

2 Cut four arch 1 (A) blanks, allowing extra length. Trace the arch 1 pattern on one piece at the proper length. Stack the four arch 1 blanks with their long edges and their bottom ends even. Clamp the stack at the bottom end to help hold it while you saw to the traced line on the band saw. Add another clamp while you sand the sawn edges.

3 With the stack separated, bevel the long edges on each arch 1 piece to 45° on the table saw. Make sure to hold the piece tight against the saw table. Find some rubber bands. Dry-assemble a square tube with the four arch 1 pieces, holding it together with the rubber bands, as shown in photo 1.

4 Cut a piece of pine for the spire (B) so that it barely slides into the assembled tube. Trace the spire shape on two adjacent sides. Use the band saw to begin sawing at the top of the spire, but don't saw all the way out the side of the workpiece. Leave a small hinge of wood, as shown in photo 2, so that the waste pieces from the first two cuts remain in place while you cut the lines on the adjacent side (see photo 3). Then break off the waste from the first two cuts.

5 Use a spokeshave and a low-angle block plane to smooth the sawn faces. Beginning 4" from the bottom of the spire, use a sharp chisel to bevel the square corners to begin an octagonal top section, as shown in photo 4. Then plane the top of the spire to an octagon, as shown in photo 5. Sand the non-square faces of the spire, keeping the corners crisp. Put a pencil mark on one side of the spire, 4⅛" from its bottom end.

6 Apply glue to the bevels on the arch 1 pieces, and reassemble them into a square tube. Use a rubber band to hold the bottom end of the tube together. Apply glue to the bottom 3½" of the spire, and separate the top ends of the arches enough to slide the spire in until your mark hits the top of an arch (see photo 6). Add more rubber bands and clamps to hold the assembly while the glue cures. Make sure the assembly is square and the corners line up accurately.

7 Now you're ready to add successive arch layers over the arch 1 assembly. If your plywood is not exactly ⅜" and ½" thick, or is not the same thickness everywhere, which is very likely, you will have to adjust the widths of the remaining mitered arches (C–G). A prudent worker would fit the next pieces to the already-glued ones in any case, right? You should also line up the arch patterns with each edge of the blanks to trace them, so that the curves blend into the sides, even when the blanks are narrower than the pattern. Cut the pieces for arch 2 (C), trace your pattern, saw out the parts, and sand as before. Then bevel the edges on the table saw to fit tightly around the arch 1 assembly.

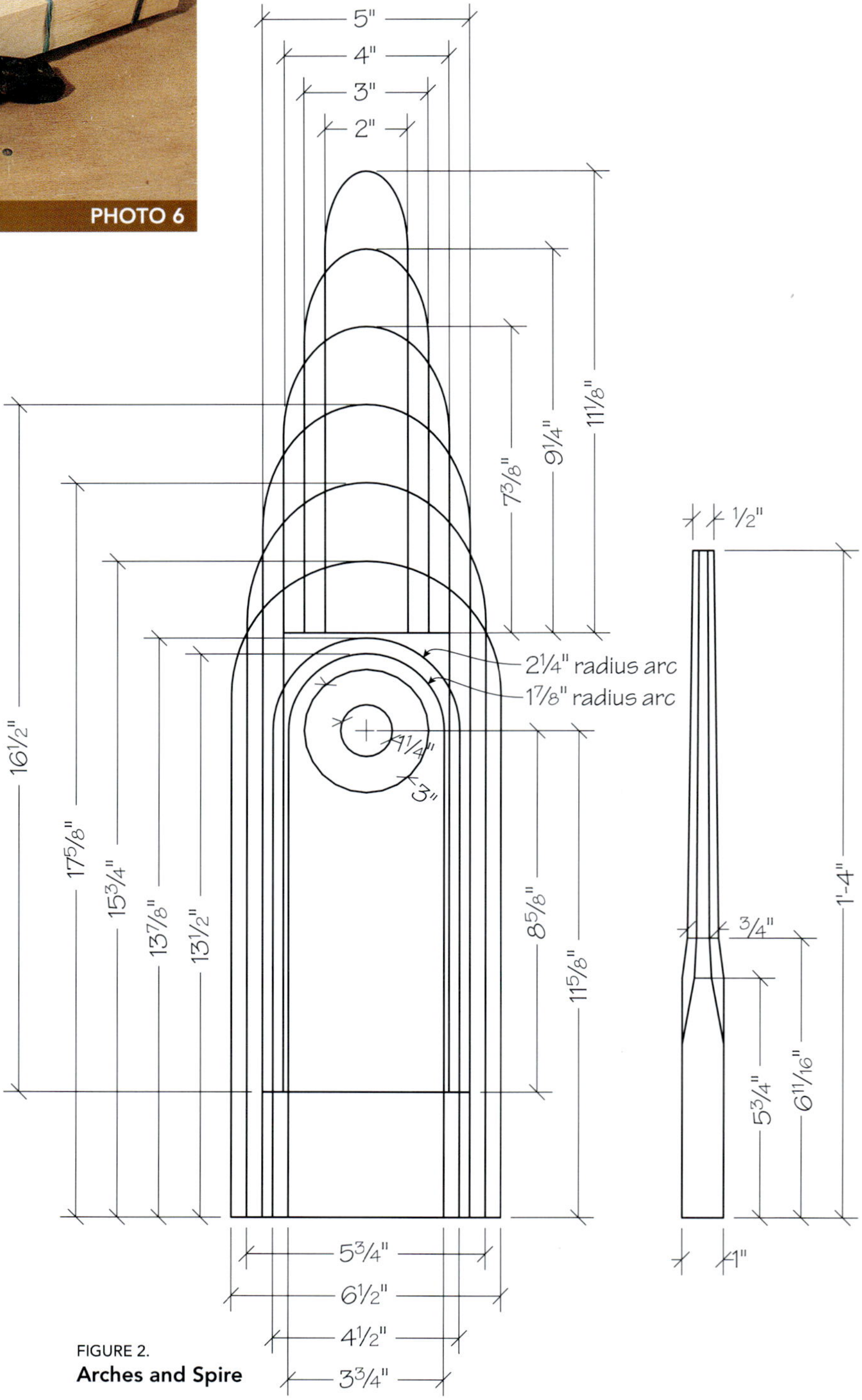

FIGURE 2.
Arches and Spire

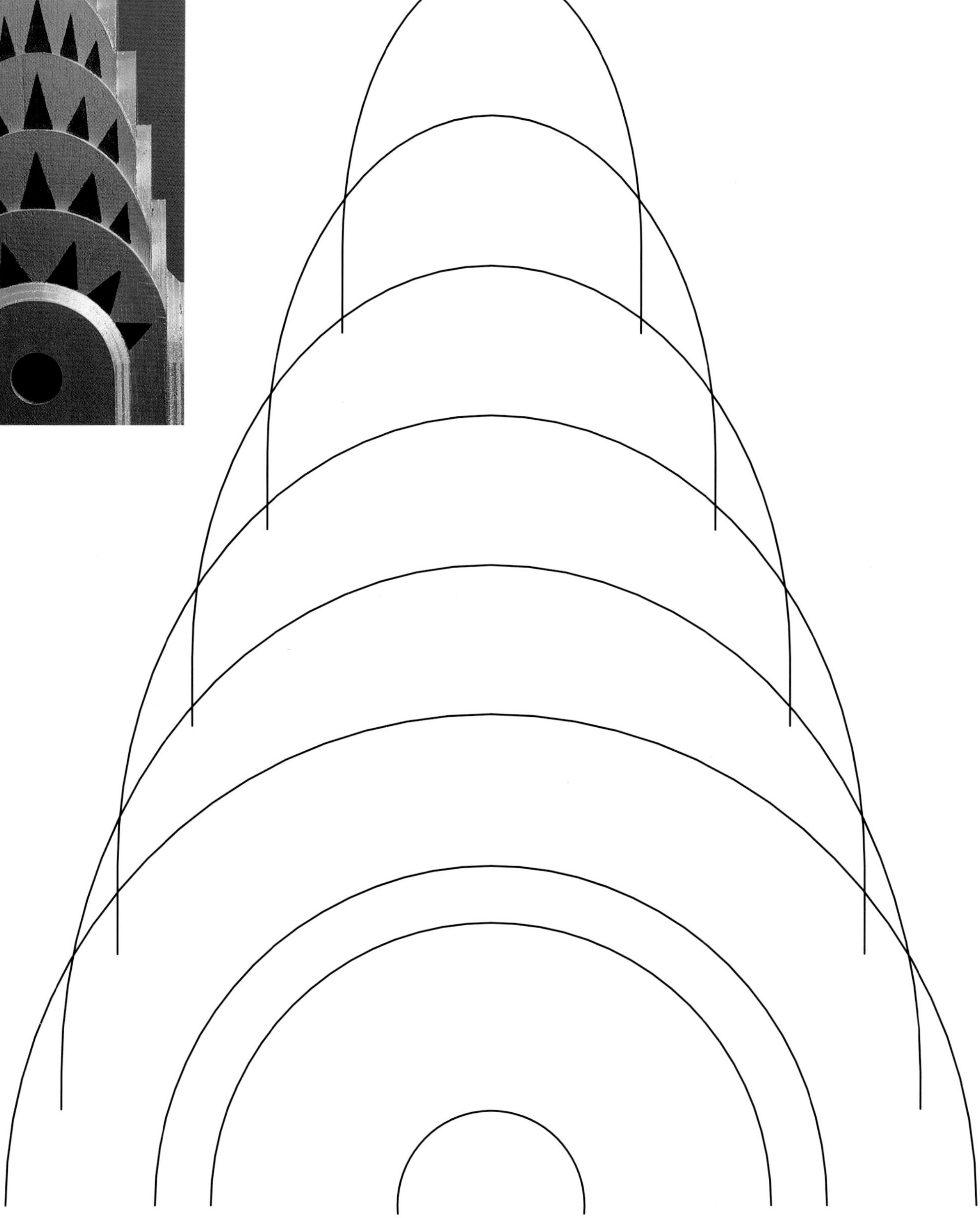

FIGURE 3. **Arch Patterns**

8 Spread glue over the inside faces and bevels of the arch 2 pieces, and press them into place. Hold them tight with rubber bands and clamps as necessary. The bottom ends of arch 2 should be even with the bottom ends of arch 1. The distance between the tops of the arches should be 1⅞", as is the case with each set of arches except for arch 8.

9 Prepare and assemble the pieces for arch 3 (D) in the same way as for arch 2.

10 Prepare the arch 4 (E) pieces. Drill a 3" hole through one of the arch 4 pieces, centered 8⅝" from its bottom end. Then glue up and clamp as before, positioning arch 4 1⅞" below arch 3, and making sure that the bottom ends of arch 4 are even. (See photo 7.)

ADDING THE LOWER ARCHES AND FLOOR

1 Cut out pieces for arch 5 (F) from ⅜" plywood, with a 3" hole centered 11⅝" from the bottom of one piece, and glue them as before.

2 Cut the pieces for arch 6 (G), but don't glue them to the house yet.

3 The arch 7 (H) pieces are bevelled on the outside, including their curves, as shown in figure 1. Cut the long edge bevels as before, and trace the curved pattern at the top of each blank. Then cut the curve with the band-saw table tilted to 45°, as shown in photo 8.

4 Arch 8 (I) has no bevelled edges, but its curve should match the smaller face of arch 7 exactly. Cut the arch 8 pieces from ¼" plywood.

5 Stack one arch 6, one arch 7, and one arch 8 together, with their bottom edges even. Open the stack enough to spread glue between the layers, rearrange them, and clamp them. When the glue has dried, drill a 1¼" hole through all three, centered 11⅝" from the bottom.

PHOTO 8

6 Glue three more stacks with the remaining arch pieces. When the glue has dried, glue and clamp all four stacks to the house.

7 Cut the floor (J) to fit over the bottoms of the arch 5 pieces. Drill one pilot hole per edge, and fasten the floor with #6 x 1⅝" decking screws. Do not glue the floor, because you will want to remove it to clean the house.

PHOTO 7

PHOTO 9

PHOTO 10

ADDING THE PLINTH

1 Glue some ½" or ¾" plywood into a 1½"-thick stack for the plinth (K). You can use other 1½" material instead, such as an unblemished 2 x 6. The plinth pieces should be ½" shorter than the width of the arch 6 pieces. Cut the plinth pieces to size.

2 Arrange the plinth as shown in figure 4. Two opposite pieces will end up flush with two faces of arch 8. Cut and glue the screw strips (L) in place, as shown in photo 9.

3 Measure the length and width of the plinth as arranged. The width measurement should be the same as the distance across the base of the tower. Glue a stack of plywood 1½" thick and cut it to the plinth measurements for the base (M). Put the plinth pieces on the base, and trace their inside faces. Drill a ½" hole near each corner of the traced rectangle, and cut to the inside of the line with a jigsaw (see photo 10).

4 Drill two pilot holes through each screw strip and into its plinth, and reinforce the glue joint with 1⅝" screws. Drill two more pilot holes through each screw strip in a vertical direction to allow for fastening the plinth to the tower.

5 Drill two pilot holes for #8 screws through the base on each side of the opening. Arrange the plinth pieces upside down on your bench, apply glue to the bottom edges, put the base on top, clamp it in place, and fasten it with 2½" screws.

6 Make sure you have a good fit between the bottom of the tower and the top of the plinth. Spread glue on the bottom end of the tower and put it in place on the plinth. Allow the glue to cure long enough to hold the pieces together, then drive 2" screws through the screw strips and into the tower.

7 Finally, make the triangular braces (N) and glue them in place, as shown in figure 1. In photo 11, I'm splitting an overlength, ½"-square piece diagonally and only partway on the table saw, with the blade tilted to 45°. For safety, hold on to the extra length and back the workpiece away from the blade before your fingers get near it, or stop the blade in the middle of the cut. Once you've positioned the braces and the glue has dried, drill 1⁄16" pilot holes and drive one 3d finish nail through each brace.

PHOTO 11

ART DECO SPLENDOR

GREAT BUILDINGS SEEM TO REQUIRE AN INSPIRED ARCHITECT and a courageous client. The Chrysler Building had both, and the result epitomized the flamboyance of the Roaring Twenties, marked the end of a high-flying era in architecture, and remains a beloved icon in New York's crowded skyline. Although Walter P. Chrysler had instructed William van Alen to make his building taller than the Eiffel Tower, its originally announced height was only 925 feet; the tower's actual height was 986 feet. Worse, in 1930 the Bank of Manhattan was finished at 927 feet and was then the tallest building in the world.

In addition to designing dramatic buildings, van Alen was a spectacular showman. He had the 27-ton spire constructed, in effective secrecy, within the fire shaft at the top of the building. On its completion, workmen hoisted the entire spire straight into the sky, increasing the building's height to 1,046 feet within weeks of its rival's completion. In 1931 the tallest building title moved to the Empire State Building, which was 204 feet higher and which retained the honor for 40 years.

The Chrysler Building frankly confronts one of the problems of skyscrapers: Their great height presents an observer with decidedly different experiences, depending on his point of view. The Chrysler Building fills its trapezoidal site at the base, modulating through a rectangle to its square plan at the top. Along the way, each successive section has its own set of automobile-inspired ornaments: hubcaps, hood ornaments, winged radiator caps, wheels, and stylized cars. Theatrical entrances invite passersby into the lavish lobby, which was originally intended to display Chrysler's new models. The building's top, visible only from a distance, shines in its cladding of Nirosta metal—a chrome-nickel stainless steel. It would attract attention for this new surface alone, but van Alen broke the reflections into a series of sunbursts pierced by triangular windows which, in turn, invoke the crown on the Statue of Liberty. That's a lot of metaphorical resonance for one building to handle!

PHOTO BY MARIJO ERZINGER, MARIJO ERZINGER PHOTOGRAPHY, WINNETKA, IL

FINISHING UP THE HOUSE

1 Sand the entire tower to remove fuzzy edges and other blemishes. Prime the tower at least once, sanding after each coat.

2 I used aluminum-colored spray paint to produce a surface as close as possible to the original without using silver leaf. Follow the directions on the can, and plan for a number of coats. The process is so easy that you'll want to build a nice, smooth surface.

3 Dig out those arch patterns again. Arrange them just as their pieces ended up on the tower, so that you can trace and cut each lower arch from the one above it. Do this to make pattern pieces to use as stencils for painting the windows. Once the arches are cut, refer to the project photos to draw triangles on the arch patterns. Cut out the triangles with a sharp craft knife and a ruler.

4 Lay the tower on kraft paper on your bench. Beginning with the top arch, hold the arch stencil tightly against the tower, and paint inside the triangles. I used Bronze Metallic acrylic paint. A "pouncing" motion with the brush works well, but don't get any paint on the top of the next arch, and try not to let paint flow under the stencil. Your paint will not cover with the first coat, so get an even coverage without applying too much acrylic.

5 Remove the first stencil as soon as you're finished with it, and go on to the next larger arch. By the time you've finished the first side, the stencils will be dry enough to begin the second side. By the time you've finished the fourth side, the first side will be ready for a second coat. Apply a second coat to all the sides and you're finished!

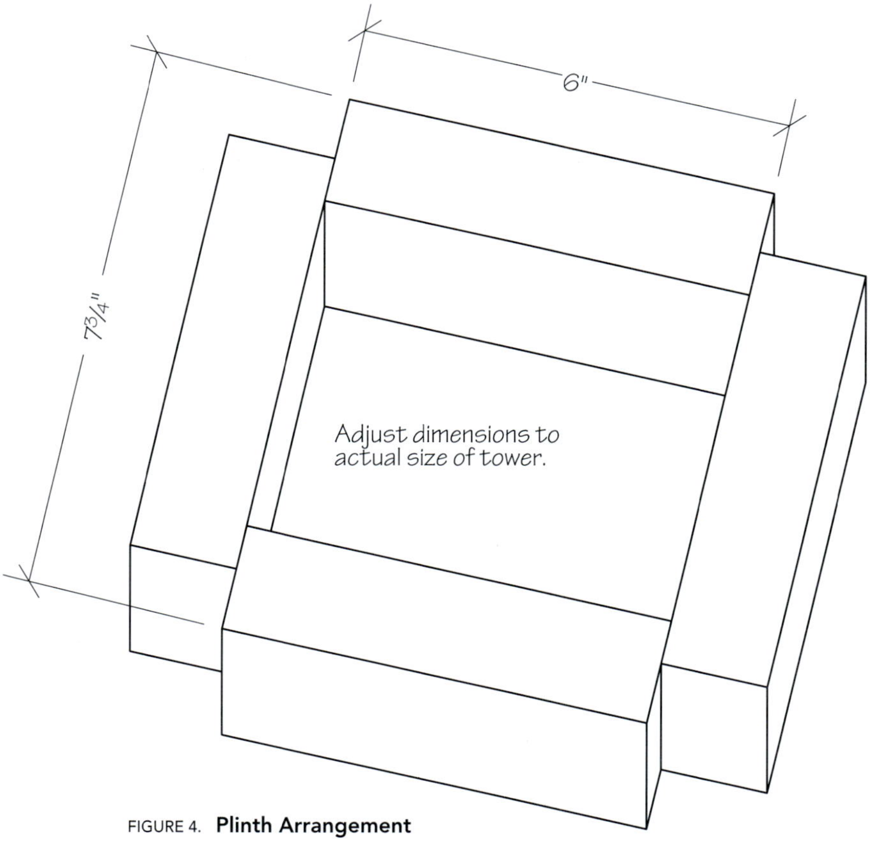

FIGURE 4. **Plinth Arrangement**

GOTHIC CATHEDRAL

PILEATED WOODPECKER HOUSE

ARCHITECT: French Master Stone-Mason

This birdhouse looks difficult to build, but it isn't. It will take some time, but not nearly the hundred years it took to build the originals. This is a grand project for a grand bird. If you have pileated woodpeckers nearby, do try to make them feel welcome.

MATERIALS

- ½" exterior plywood, ½ sheet
- ¾" exterior plywood, ¼ sheet
- Pine, 1 x 8 x 4'
- Pine, ⅜" x 2" x 2'

SUPPLIES

- ¾" brads
- 3d finishing nails
- 4d finishing nails
- #6 x 1⅝" decking screws
- 1/16" and 3/32" drill bits, ¾" spade bit, and 3½" hole saw
- #6 pilot bit
- Double-sided (carpet) tape
- Waxed paper

CUTTING LIST

CODE	DESCRIPTION	QTY.	MATERIAL	DIMENSIONS
A	Ends	3	plywood	3/4" x 8" x 19 3/4"
B	Front	1	plywood	3/4" x 19 1/4" x 20 1/2"
C	Sides	2	plywood	1/2" x 12 1/2" x 15 3/4"
D	Base	1	plywood	3/4" x 14" x 20"
E	Buttresses	10	plywood	1/2" x 5 1/8" x 15"
F	Left roof	1	plywood	1/2" x 7" x 12 1/2"
G	Right roof	1	plywood	1/2" x 6 1/2" x 12 1/2"
H	Tall pillars	6	pine	3/4" x 1" x 27 7/8"
I	Roof pillars	2	pine	3/4" x 1" x 11 1/2"
J	Tower pillars	2	pine	3/4" x 3/4" x 6 1/2"
K	Tower crosses	2	pine	3/4" x 1" x 6 1/4"
L	Center chevrons	2	pine	1/2" x 3/4" x 5 1/8"
M	Side chevrons	4	pine	1/2" x 3/4" x 4 1/2"
N	Lower cross	1	pine	3/8" x 3/4" x 20"
O	Upper crosses	2	pine	3/8" x 3/8" x 20"

FIGURE 1. **Gothic Cathedral Pileated Woodpecker House**

PHOTO 1

PHOTO 2

PHOTO 3

MAKING THE WALLS AND BUTTRESSES

1 Cut the three ends (A), using the dimensions in figure 2. Use a stop on the miter gauge of your table saw to cut the 45° top angles, as shown in photos 1 and 2. Trim ½" from the peaks of the ends, as shown, for ventilation. Cut the rectangular piece for the front (B), as well.

2 Stack one end on the back side of the front, centering it widthwise and keeping their bottom edges flush. Drive a few 3d finishing nails to keep the two pieces aligned. Mark the center for the entrance hole, 13¾" above the bottom of the pieces, as shown in figure 2. You can cut this hole with a 3½" hole saw if you happen to have one lying around, but it's probably easier to cut the hole with a jigsaw. Use a compass to draw a 3½" circle on the end, then bore a ¾" hole within the circle to provide a starting place for the saw. (See photo 3, in which I have just finished the cut.) Saw to the line. Clean up the saw marks, using a rasp and 100-grit sandpaper.

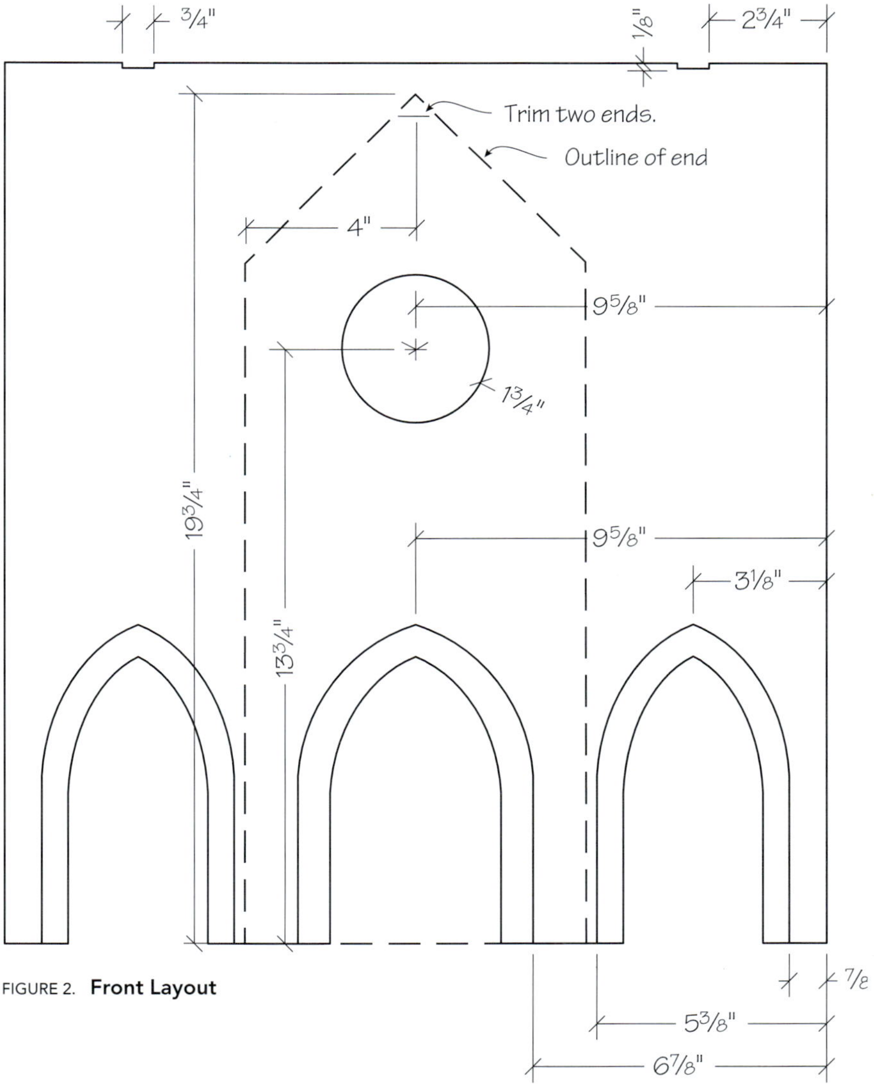

FIGURE 2. **Front Layout**

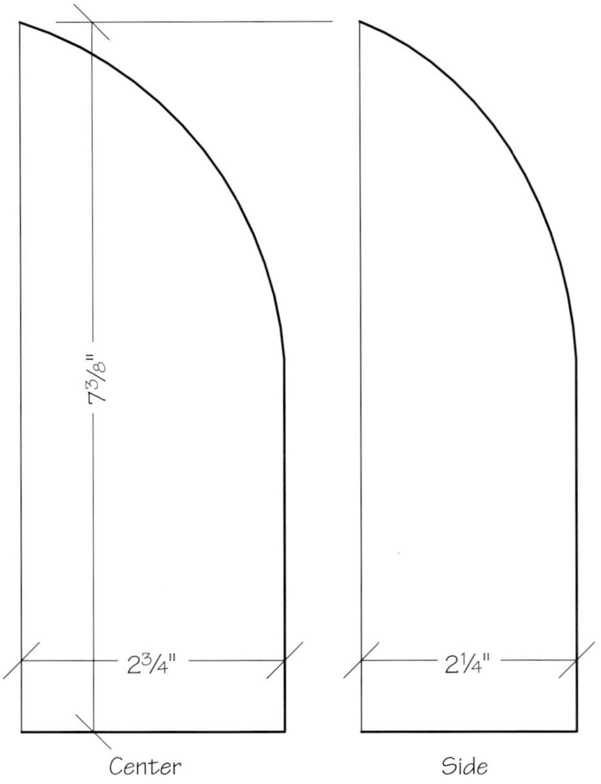

FIGURE 3. **Entrance Half-Patterns**

PHOTO 4

PHOTO 5

3 Referring to figure 3, make two patterns for the center and side entrances in the front. The patterns should represent the heavier, outside lines of the openings. Make your patterns from heavy paper folded on the vertical centerline to make sure that the two sides will be symmetrical. Check to make sure that the patterns are exactly 5½" and 4½" wide.

4 Carefully pry the front from the end and remove the nails. Place your entrance patterns precisely as shown in figure 2, and use a sharp pencil to trace them onto the plywood. You can cut most of the outline using a jigsaw, and finish the peak of the arch with a coping saw. Begin with the center entrance. Tilt the base of your jigsaw to 45°. Cut close to the line on the waste side (inside the line), as shown in photo 4. Avoid exerting any sideways pressure on the blade. When you're close to the peak—perhaps 1" away—begin turning to pick up the line on the other side, then finish the cut. Use a coping saw to cut to the peak of the arch, being careful to avoid cutting past the center on the back side.

5 To cut the side entrance arches, tilt the base of the jigsaw to 40°, and proceed as for the center arch. You will need to begin the turn earlier in the cut because the side arches are narrower. If the blade begins to bind, back off and start your turn earlier. Finish the cut with a coping saw and a sharp chisel, as shown in photo 5. Use a rasp or a file and sandpaper to smooth the arches. Make the miter line at the peak nice and crisp.

PHOTO 6

PHOTO 7

PHOTO 8

6 Cut the sides (C), making sure that the bevel at the top aligns with the angled roofline of the ends. You might use one of the ends to set your rip fence, as shown in photo 6. Then cut out the base (D).

7 From ½" plywood, cut 10 pieces, each 5⅛" wide and at least 15" long. Make sure that one end of each piece, which will be the bottom of the buttresses (E), is square to the long edges.

8 Using figure 4, draw and cut a pattern for the buttresses from heavy paper or mat board. Making a 200 percent photocopy of figure 4 is the most direct road to a good pattern, but you can easily draw the pattern, too.

9 Make stacks of two or three buttress pieces each, with double-sided tape between the layers. Make sure that the long edges and square ends align perfectly. Trace the pattern onto the top piece of each stack. Use a band saw to cut away all the nonenclosed areas of the buttresses, as shown in photo 7.

10 Drill a ¾" hole inside each of the enclosed areas of the buttresses. Use a jigsaw to cut out the rest of the waste (see photo 8). Clean up and fair all the sawn edges of the buttresses, using a rasp and 100-grit sandpaper. Keep the edges square to the surfaces—don't round them over! Ease the corners with sandpaper, but leave the corners that will touch the sides alone.

11 A word to the reader willing to learn from experience: You would be very wise, as I was not, to prime and paint the buttresses now. Just leave bare the edges that will touch the sides and the base.

PHOTO 9

ASSEMBLING THE WALLS AND BUTTRESSES

1 Make a mark on each side to designate its back edge. On the outside of each side, use the dimensions in figure 5 to draw vertical lines representing the back faces of the buttresses. The last buttress will be flush with the back of the cathedral (actually, the altar end, which is traditionally the east end, but we will stick to birdhouse reality). While you're there, draw another vertical line 3⅜" from each back edge, and drill four 1⁄16" pilot holes, evenly distributed along that line, through each side.

2 More marking out! Turn those sides over, and draw the vertical and horizontal lines shown in figure 5. Isn't this fun? Use a pen to draw vertical lines 3" and 3¾" from the back edge. That's where the divider goes.

3 Working on the base, clamp a side to the edges of two ends to hold the side vertical, as shown in photo 9. Apply glue to the edges of a buttress where they meet a side, and press the buttress into place, with its back face at one of the lines you drew in step 1. Hold the buttress firmly until the glue begins to set. Glue four more buttresses to the side in the same way.

PHOTO 10

PHOTO 11

PHOTO 12

PHOTO 13

4 When the glue has dried, drill a pilot hole for a #6 screw, through the side and into each lower buttress connection at the intersections of the lines you drew in step 2, as shown in photo 10. Drive 1⅝" screws to reinforce the glued joints.

5 Repeat steps 3 and 4 to fasten the remaining buttresses to the other side.

6 Still working on the base, apply glue to a vertical edge of the end with the entrance hole, and clamp the appropriate side flush to the end. Drill four 1/16" pilot holes through the joint, and drive 3d nails, as shown in photo 11.

7 Apply glue to an edge of one of the remaining ends, and clamp it in place between the pen lines you drew in step 2. Drive 3d finishing nails through the pilot holes from step 1.

8 Fasten the remaining end at the back of the side, drilling 1/16" pilot holes where you can between the buttress arms, as shown in photo 12.

9 Apply glue to the opposite edges of the ends, and clamp the other side in place. Drill pilot holes, and reinforce the joints with finishing nails as before (see photo 13).

10 Reinforce the upper buttress arms by drilling angled 1/16" pilot holes and driving 3d nails, as shown in photo 14.

PHOTO 14

ADDING THE ROOF, FRONT, AND BASE

1 Cut ½" plywood for the left roof (F) and the right roof (G). Apply glue to the top edge of the right roof, and clamp the left roof to that edge. You can do this most conveniently by using the ends to support the roof pieces, as shown in photo 15. Make sure that the top edge of the left roof is flush with the outside surface of the right roof.

2 Drill four angled 1⁄16" pilot holes through the roof joint. Then drive 3d nails and set their heads to secure the two roof pieces to each other. When the glue has set, remove the roof from the wall assembly.

3 Working on the base, with waxed paper placed between the glue and the base, apply glue to the front end, avoiding the open area on the front, and press the front against it. Make sure the holes align perfectly and that the bottom edges of the walls and the front are standing on the base. Clamp the front to the end at the top in two places. When you are sure that nothing will slide around, tilt the assembly onto the back end so that you can clamp the bottom of the front to the front end.

4 When the glue has cured and the clamps are off, place the cathedral assembly in position on the base, centered widthwise, with the front ¾" from the front edge of the base. Use a piece of your pine stock to gauge the offset. Trace around all the pieces touching the base, inside and out. Remove the cathedral. Use the #6 pilot bit to drill through the base from the top, within the traced lines: four holes for the front, two for each end, and three for each side. Turn the base over, and, in each pilot hole, drill a countersink just deep enough for the screw head.

5 Replace the cathedral on the top face of the base. Move the front of the base past the edge of your bench, just enough to let you extend the pilot holes into the front. Turn the cathedral on its back, and apply glue to all the edges that will contact the base. Quickly put the base in position, and drive 1⅝" screws into the pilot holes you just drilled. Extend the rest of the pilot holes, and drive screws into them as well. Finally, drill 1⁄16" pilot holes through the base and into the outer buttress ends. Drive 4d nails to help secure the buttresses.

DECORATING THE FRONT

1 Go ahead and rip out enough pine stock for the rest of the pieces (H–O) to be added to the front, but don't cut them to length yet.

2 Cut notches ¾" wide and ⅛" deep in the top edge of the front, centered 3⅛" from each side as shown in figure 2. Use a handsaw to cut the ends of each notch and a sharp chisel to pare out the waste, as shown in photo 16.

3 Cut the tower pillars (J) and tower crosses (K) to length. Square lines around the tower crosses, 2¾" from each end. These lines should be ¾" apart, and they should mark the joint with the top ends of the tower pillars. Drill two 1⁄16" holes, spaced diagonally within the ¾" space, through each tower cross. Clamp a tower pillar to the bench so that you can hold a tower cross against it while you drive 4d nails through the pilot holes and into the pillar, as shown in photo 17. Set the heads, then repeat to join the other pillar and cross.

PHOTO 15

PHOTO 16

PHOTO 17

REVELATORY STRUCTURE

PHOTO BY GAYLN C. HAMMOND, HAMMOND PHOTOGRAPHY, MONTEREY, CA

THE COMBINATION OF THREE STRUCTURAL INNOVATIONS allowed Gothic architects to design a new kind of building: the pointed arch, the ribbed vault, and the buttress, all of which had been used before—but never together. These building elements enabled architects to enclose taller, more varied spaces and, at the same time, to invite more light into them. Walking into a new Gothic cathedral would have been a startling experience had not its parishioners been allowed the time to get used to it during its century or more of construction.

Pointed arches of the same height can span various distances, so the bays between columns could have different widths, as is true on the front of our birdhouse. The pointed arch also gave a greater sense of verticality than the round Romanesque arch. Supporting vaulted ceilings with ribs, instead of relying on the accumulated masonry of an arched or corbel vault, allowed builders to transfer the weight of the ceiling onto columns, eliminating the need for solid walls. This meant that windows could be much larger, allowing more light into the sanctuary, and providing larger canvases for stained-glass artisans. Finally, using buttresses to resist the tendency of walls to buckle under the weight of the roof meant that the walls could be thinner. And thinner walls can be built taller. Flying buttresses eliminated even more mass by spreading the forces bearing on the walls even farther.

Gothic architects emphasized the structure of the building with carefully articulated moldings, which followed the outlines of the arches and the ribs, and often continued down the columns. In addition to its characteristic qualities of height and light, and the dazzling maze of ornament and stained glass, the Gothic cathedral revealed its structure to an unprecedented extent. The forces working to hold up the building can be followed from floor to ceiling, with every piece having its part to play. By calling attention to itself in this way, the cathedral invited meditation on human dynamism in the act of celebrating God's glory.

PHOTO 18

PHOTO 19

4 Hold one of the pillars with its bottom end in one of the notches, flush with the front and back of the front. Drill an angled 1⁄16" pilot hole from each side of the pillar into the front, as shown in photo 18. Drive 3d nails through the pilot holes, and set the heads. Repeat with the other pillar in the other notch.

5 Cut the tall pillars (H) to length—the distance from the base to the top of the tower crosses. Run a line of glue 1⁄4" from the edge on the front and back faces of one side of the front (B). Put a drop of glue on the front and back of the outboard end of the tower cross. Clamp two tall pillars on either side of the front, such that they protrude 3⁄8" from the edge of the front and from the end of the tower cross, as shown in photo 19. Repeat with two more tall pillars on the other side of the front.

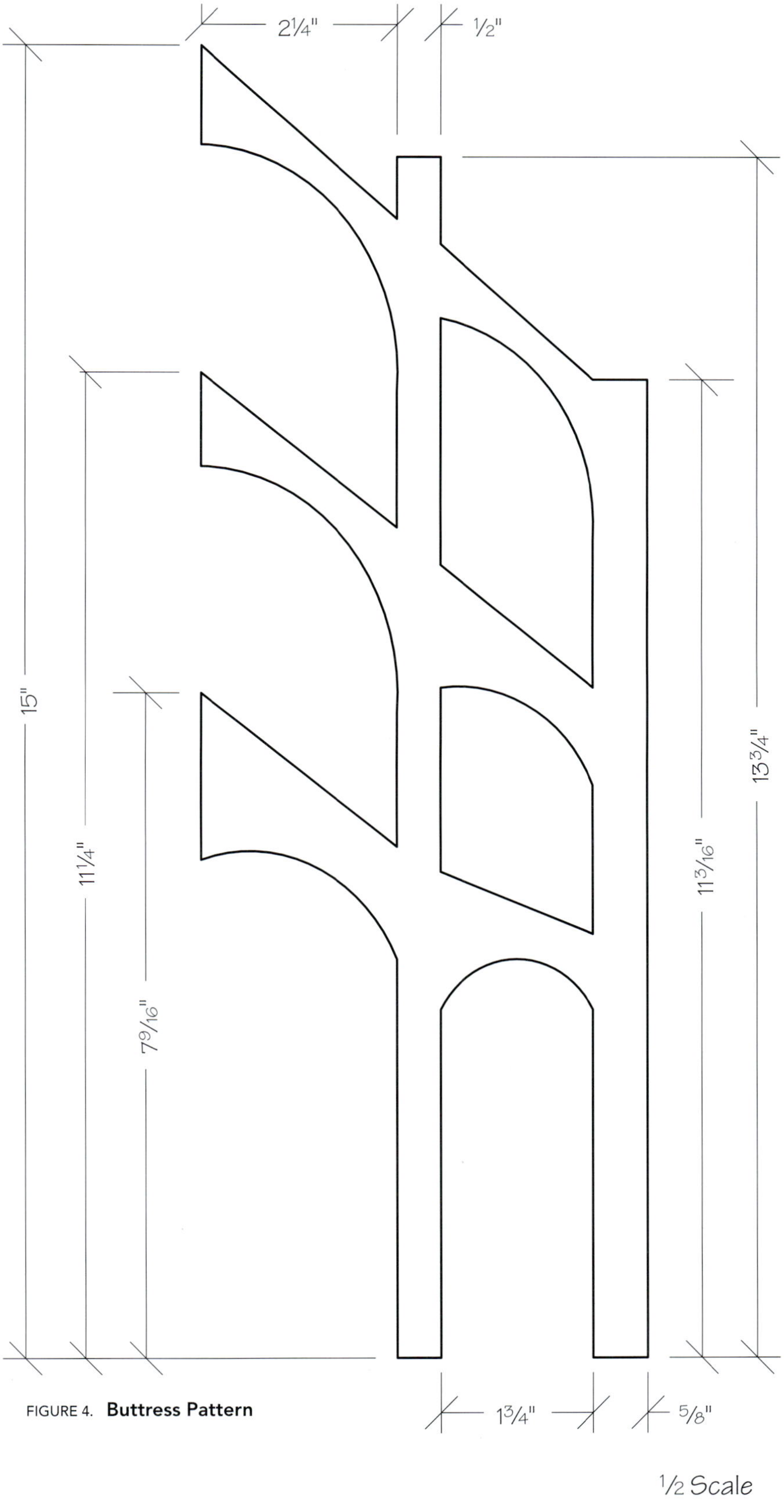

FIGURE 4. **Buttress Pattern**

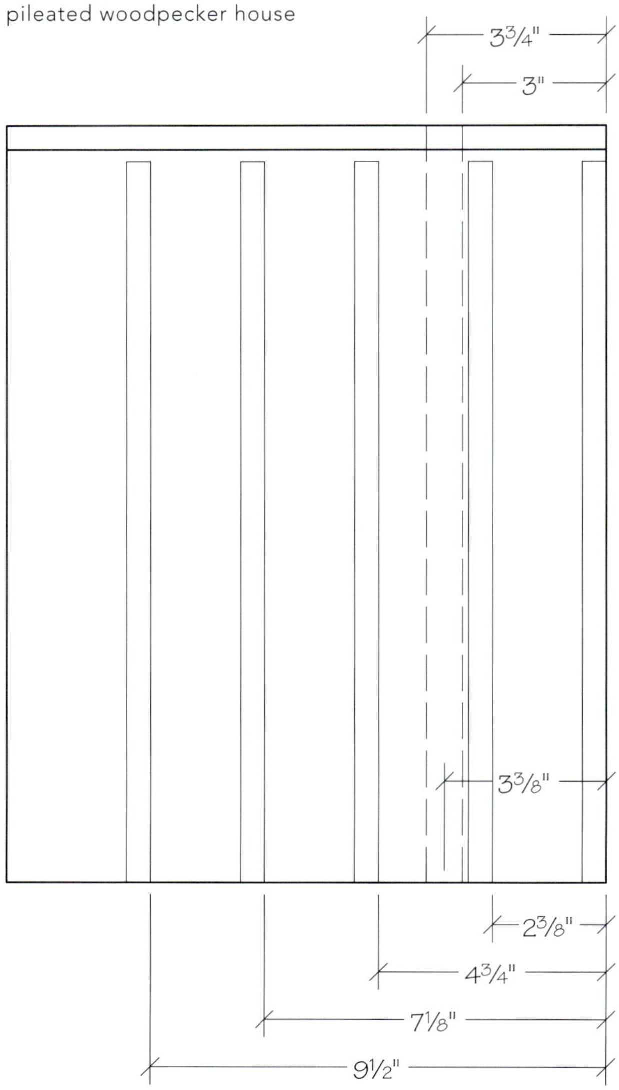

FIGURE 5. **Right Side Layout**

6 The other two tall pillars are centered between the entrance arches, as shown in figure 6. They must also protrude ⅜" from the inboard ends of the tower crosses. Lay each tall pillar in place, and trace it on the front and on the tower cross. Apply glue within the traced lines, and clamp the tall pillars in place.

7 The roof pillars (I) run behind the central pillars you just glued, between the roof and the top of the tower cross. They also hold the front end of the roof in place, so put the roof on the cathedral, and cut miters on the ends of two pieces of pillar stock, leaving them at least 12" long for now. Clamp the roof pillars in place with spring clamps, and check their alignment. Make sure that the roof can slide back for cleaning the nest cavity. Trace the pillars' positions on the back of the front, unclamp them, apply glue to the traced areas, and clamp the pillars back in place. Check the roof clearance again. When the glue has dried, you can cut off the excess pillar above the cross with a handsaw.

8 Turn the cathedral on its back end to make fitting the rest of the front decoration easier. Refer to figure 6. The ends of the center and side chevron pieces (L and M) are cut at 50° angles, which must be done by hand. So get out your bevel gauge, and use a protractor to set it to 50° from square. Mark the centerlines between the tall pillars to show where the peak of the chevrons should lie. Also mark the inside faces of the tall pillars, 5⅜" from the base for the bottom points of the chevron pieces. Cut the bottom end of each chevron piece, and press that end in place against its pillar to mark its other end from the centerline. Then square across the wider faces of the chevron piece, and saw the angle.

9 When all the chevron pieces have been cut and fitted, trace them onto the front. Apply glue to the backs of the chevron pieces and to their ends, and press them back in place. Hold them firmly until the glue begins to set.

10 Take this opportunity to clean up and sand the front, pillars, and chevrons. Round the corners of all pieces a little bit. Mark the locations of the bottom edges of the lower cross (N) and one of the upper crosses (O) on the tall pillars by measuring 10⅝" and 16⅛" from the base. The other upper cross aligns with the top of the front. Refer to figure 6.

11 Leave the crosses overlong to reduce your alignment problems. Put a drop of glue on the tall pillars, where the upper and lower crosses will go. Where you can, use spring clamps to hold the crosses to the pillars around the edges of the front. When the glue has set, drive ¾" brads through all the joints to reinforce them, and trim the ends of the crosses, as shown in photo 20.

12 One more housekeeping item: With the roof in place, drill countersunk pilot holes for #6 screws through the roof and into the back end. Use 1⅝" screws to hold the roof in place; just remove the screws to clean the nesting area.

FIGURE 6.
Front Trim Layout

PHOTO 20

PAINTING THE CATHEDRAL

1 Coat every exterior surface with a good-quality exterior primer. It would be a very good idea to prime the plywood edges first and sand them when dry, before priming the whole cathedral. Remember to remove the roof to keep from painting it closed.

2 Paint the house. You may want to choose a color that approximates the glowing stone of the original cathedrals.

DUOMO
DOUBLE FINCH HOUSE

ARCHITECT: Filippo Brunelleschi

If you've ever glanced at a picture of Florence, you've seen *il Duomo di Santa Maria del Fiore*, the dome of the Florence Cathedral. So central to the identity of the city is the Duomo that the Florentine phrase for home-sickness translates literally as "sick for the dome." For historians of architecture, the Renaissance began in 1418 with Brunelleschi's design for the Duomo. The dome was built with an entirely new construction method, and this birdhouse project may introduce you to some new techniques, too. Careful workmanship will be more important than special skills, and fitting the last vault in the dome will give you great satisfaction. The individual pieces of this project—even the laminated, curved blanks for the vaults—are not difficult to make, so forge ahead. Along the way, you'll learn to use a special jig to ease several otherwise-difficult steps.

MATERIALS

- 1/8" bending plywood, 1/4 sheet
- 1/4" exterior plywood, 1/8 sheet
- 3/8" exterior plywood, 1/8 sheet
- 1/2" exterior plywood, 1/8 sheet
- Pine, 1 x 4 x 6'

SUPPLIES

- 3d finishing nails
- #6 x 1 1/4" decking screws
- 1/16" drill bit and 1 1/4" Forstner bit
- #6 pilot bit
- Plastic masking tape
- 4 mil. plastic sheet

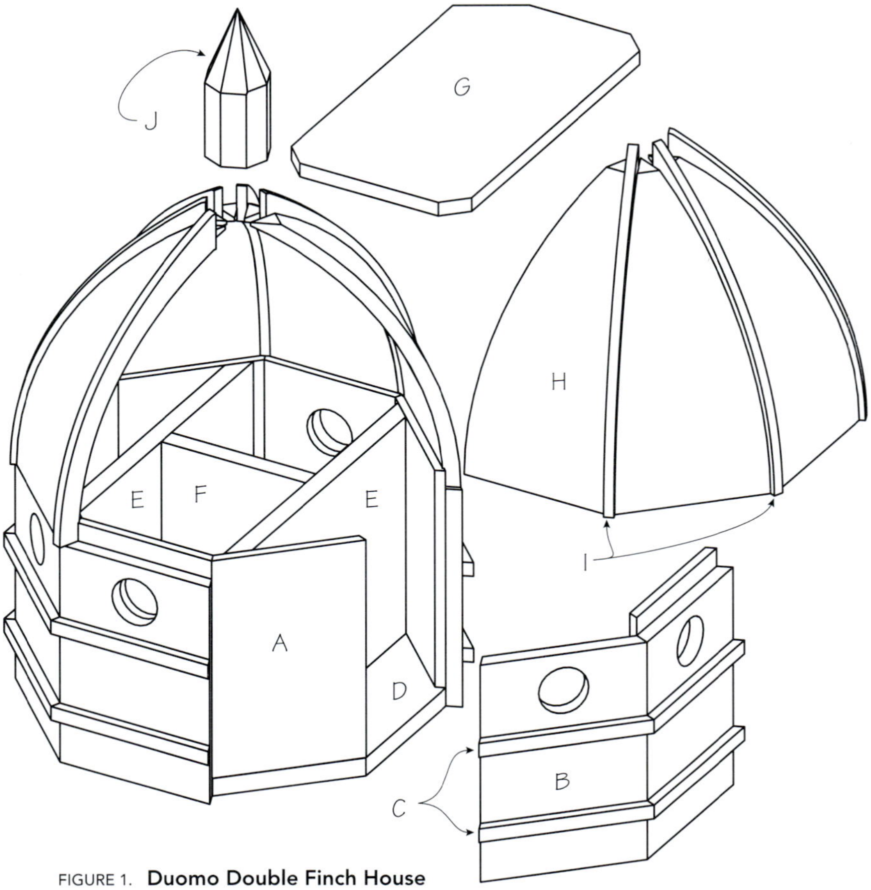

FIGURE 1. **Duomo Double Finch House**

CUTTING LIST

CODE	DESCRIPTION	QTY.	MATERIAL	DIMENSIONS
A	Inner walls	8	plywood	1/4" x 3 3/4" x 6"
B	Outer walls	8	plywood	3/8" x 4 1/8" x 6"
C	Banding	16	pine	1/4" x 3/8" x 4 3/8"
D	Floor	1	plywood	1/2" x 9 1/4" x 9 1/4"
E	Partitions	2	plywood	1/2" x 6" x 8 1/4"
F	Divider	1	plywood	1/2" x 4 1/4" x 6"
G	Ceiling	1	plywood	3/8" x 5 1/4" x 9 1/4"
H	Vaults*	8	plywood	3/8" x 4" x 9 1/4"
I	Ribs	8	pine	1/4" x 2 3/4" x 9"
J	Lantern	1	pine	1 1/2" x 1 1/2" x 4"

* Each made from three pieces of 1/8" bending plywood glued together

PHOTO 1

PHOTO 2

PHOTO 3

PHOTO 4

ERECTING THE WALLS

1 To make a complicated job easier, we'll glue the stock for the walls (A and B) and the banding (C) together before we cut their miter joints. Cut one 6" x 40" piece each from ¼" and ⅜" plywood for the inner and outer walls. Rip two pieces of pine banding, each 40" long. Use figure 2 to help lay out the positions of the holes, banding, and cutting lines on the outer wall stock, and number the areas as shown.

2 Bore the holes through the outer wall in areas 2, 3, 4, 6, 7, and 8, as indicated in figure 2.

3 Glue the inner wall stock to the back of the outer wall stock, so that the inner wall protrudes ½" above the outer wall, as shown in photo 1. Be sure to use plenty of clamps, and clamp the sandwich to a flat surface so that you don't make a bent wall. There'll be plenty of curves later in this project—we don't need to start dealing with them just yet.

4 Glue the banding in place on the outer wall.

5 Bore entrance holes through the outer and inner walls in areas 1 and 5.

6 With the table-saw blade tilted to 22.5°, use the miter gauge to cut to the lines on the right-hand side of each numbered area, as shown in photo 2. (You will have the top of the wall assembly against your miter gauge if your saw tilts the opposite way from mine.)

7 Turn each piece 180°, and set the rip fence to cut to the other line. Cut all eight wall pieces against the rip fence, as shown in photo 3. For safety, remove each piece from the saw table before you cut the next one.

8 Here's a trick to make gluing the walls easier: Align all the wall pieces with the points of the banding touching. Use high-quality plastic masking tape on the banding to hold the pieces in place (see photo 4). Press the tape down firmly. Before proceeding one step further, go get your band clamps or giant rubber bands—and a helper. Carefully flip the whole mess upside down. Put glue in the joints, as shown in photo 5. Roll the wall pieces into an octagon, stand it upright on your bench, and clamp it together. Measure across from corner to corner (four ways, remember) to make sure the octagon is regular, as shown in photo 6. Wasn't that fun?

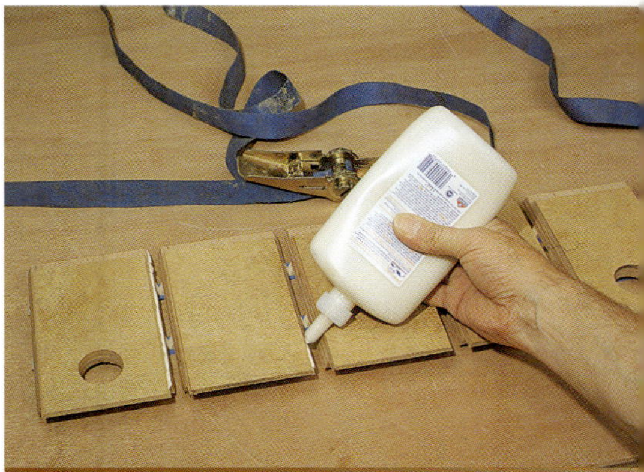
PHOTO 5

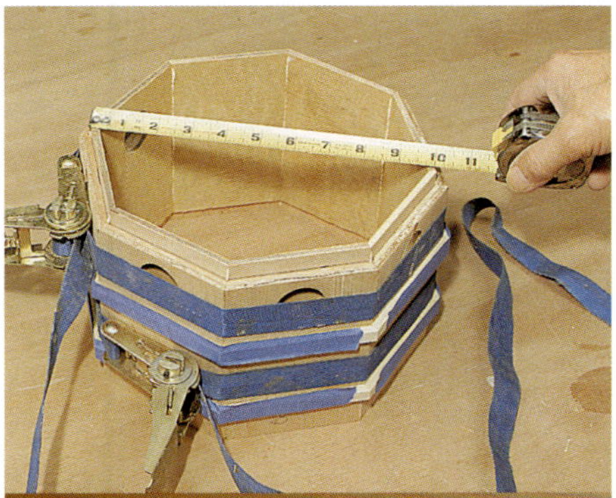
PHOTO 6

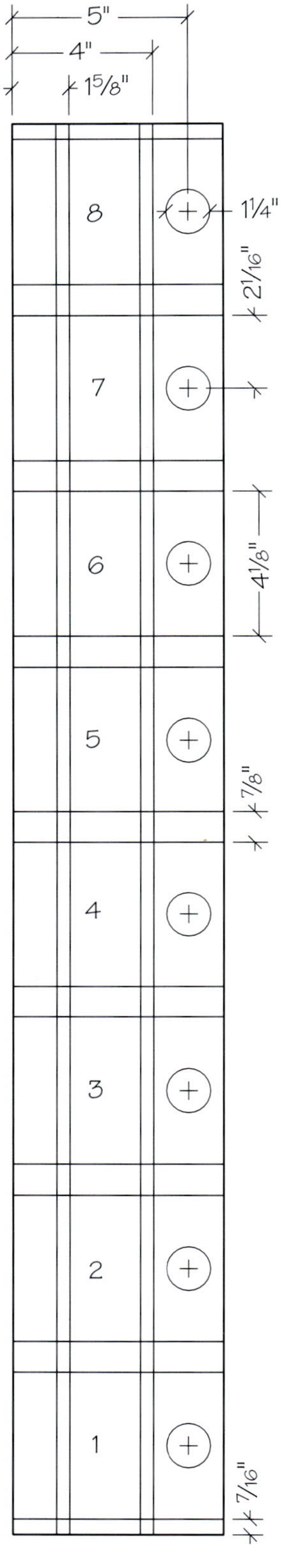

FIGURE 2. **Wall Layout**

COMPLETING THE BASE

1 When the glue has dried, put the octagon on a piece of ½" plywood, and trace the inside faces of the outer walls. Cut the floor (D) to the traced lines, using the table saw or band saw.

2 Cut the partitions (E) to size, with opposing 45° miters on their ends, as shown in figure 3. Put the octagon in place around the floor. Place the partitions against the insides of the walls next to those with the entrance holes. Arrange the partitions evenly against the walls, at right angles to the entrance walls.

3 Measure the distance between the partitions and cut the divider (F) to that width. Push the divider into place between the partitions to check your accuracy.

4 Remove the partitions and the divider. Clamp the divider between the centers of the partitions. Drill two #6 pilot holes per joint, then glue and screw the partitions to the divider.

5 Replace the partitions and divider in the octagon. Drill 1/16" pilot holes—three per joint—and drive 3d finishing nails to secure the octagon to the partitions, as shown in photo 7. Don't drive any nails into the floor! Because of the angled sides, you'll have to drive the last bit of each nail with the nail set.

6 Trace the partitions onto the floor. Remove the floor and drill three #6 pilot holes within the space marked for each partition. Countersink the pilot holes from the bottom of the floor. Turn the base assembly over, replace the floor, extend the pilot holes into the partitions, and drive 1¼" screws. Don't glue the floor; you'll want to remove it to clean the nesting boxes.

7 Cut the ceiling (G) to fit over the partitions and the inner walls, to close the nesting areas. In photo 8, I'm tracing the inner walls onto the ceiling. The ceiling should not extend past the inner walls at all. Drill pilot holes through the ceiling into the partitions, then glue and screw the ceiling in place. Remember to run a narrow line of glue along the top edges of the walls where the ceiling will land.

PHOTO 7

PHOTO 8

FIGURE 3.
Partitions

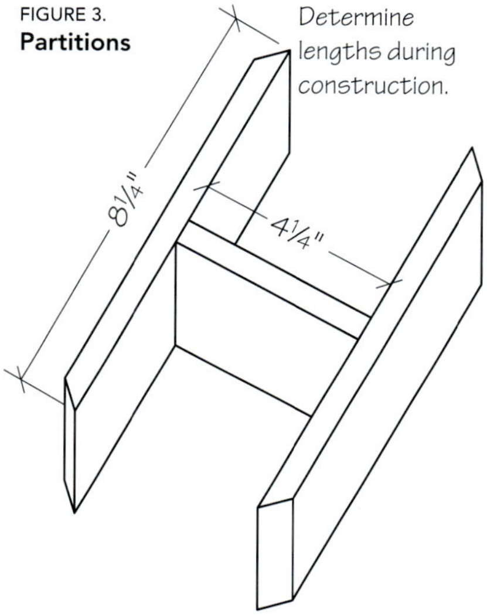

MAKING THE VAULTS AND RIBS

1 It's time to laminate the curved vaults (H), but don't worry—it's easier than it looks. From a stack of plywood 4½" thick, lay out and cut a two-part mold on the band saw, as detailed in figure 4. If you saw carefully to the lines, you won't need to smooth the sawn surfaces. You must saw both lines, however, to leave a ⅜" space between the parts of the mold (see photo 9). Staple or tape a piece of plastic sheet to each part of the mold to keep the vaults from sticking to it.

2 Cut 24 pieces of ⅛" bending plywood, each 4¼" x 10". Bending plywood bends more easily in one direction than in the other, so make sure your pieces are aligned correctly.

3 The best adhesive for laminating is structural epoxy. It's expensive, needs mixing, and takes six hours to cure. If you want your duomo birdhouse to last as long as the one in Florence, use structural epoxy. The rest of us will use regular exterior woodworking glue and be done this week. Spread a thin layer of glue on each surface inside your stack, to ensure that the joint will not be starved, but don't use so much glue that it will take forever to dry. Use a waste stick to spread the glue evenly, as I'm doing in photo 10. Glue up a stack of three pieces of bending plywood, center it between the parts of the mold, and clamp the mold together. Make sure that the layers are even with each other and that the sides of the stack are parallel with the sides of the mold. Use six clamps or more, spaced in pairs, to exert pressure evenly on the laminate, as shown in photo 11.

4 Laminate seven more vault blanks.

5 While you're waiting for the glue to dry, you can prepare the rest of the pieces for the dome. Make a rib pattern from the information in figure 5. (See Making Patterns on page 14 for some useful tips.)

6 The pattern drawing shows the rib ends landing on opposing miter cuts. Prepare the stock for the ribs (I), and use the table saw to cut the 45° angles, as shown in figure 5.

PHOTO 13

PHOTO 14

PHOTO 15

7 Trace the rib pattern on two pieces of the stock. Make two stacks with the pattern pieces on top, and tape the mitered ends together. Cut to the lines on the band saw, as shown in photo 12. You'll have to move the tape after cutting the first side. Smooth the saw cuts with sandpaper or a small spokeshave, and use a low-angle block plane for the convex curves, as I'm doing in photo 13.

PHOTO 16

FIGURE 4. **Vault Mold**

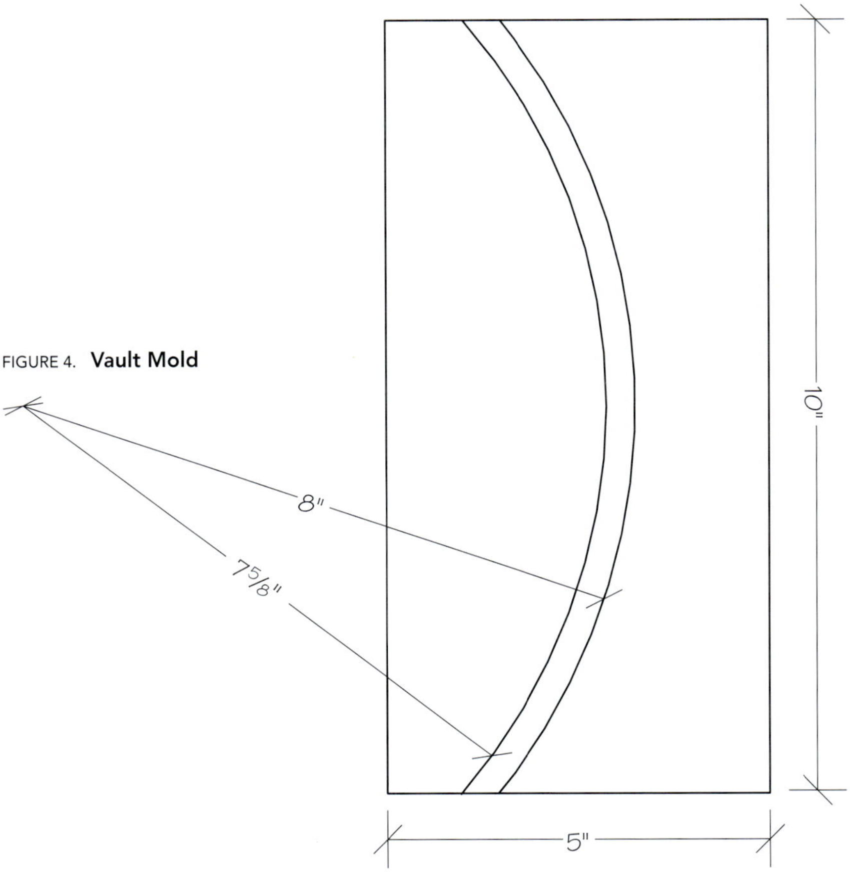

8 To make the lantern (J), prepare an overlong 1½" x 1½" x 4" square. Rip off its corners to form a regular octagon, as shown in photo 14, then trim it to 4" long. Find the center of the top, and plane an octagonal pyramid on the top half of the lantern, using a low-angle block plane (see photos 15 and 16).

9 We'll make a multi-purpose jig to help shape the vaults. Since this jig affects every step in preparing the vaults, you must make it accurately. Refer to figure 5 again, and use the inside curve of the rib pattern to mark and cut two pieces of ¼" plywood in the shape of the shaded area that's marked "vaulting jig." The material you use for these two pieces must be ¼" thick, or your jig won't be accurate. If your plywood is thin, glue enough veneer to one surface to make it at least ¼" thick.

PHOTO 17

PHOTO 18

PHOTO 19

PHOTO 20

PHOTO 21

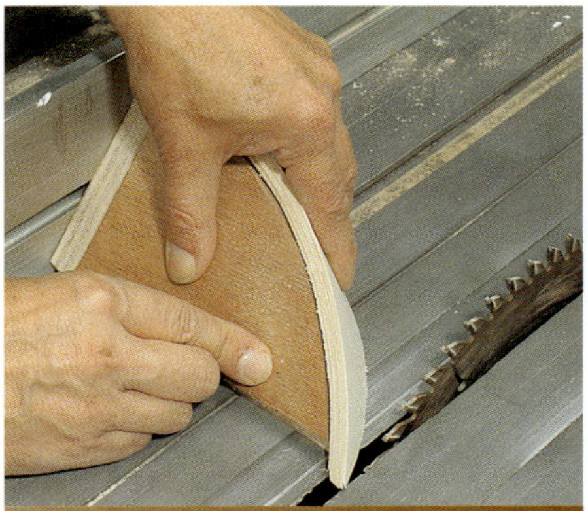
PHOTO 22

10 Saw three 45° wedges from scrap ½" or ¾" plywood, as shown in photo 17. Glue the ¼" pieces to the sides of one wedge so that the inside corners of their vertical edges meet at the point of the wedge, as shown in photo 18. Tape the vertical edges together, then cut the wedge even with the curved edges of the ¼" pieces (see photo 19).

11 Put the jig on the second of the three wedges, aligning it with the outside faces of the ¼" pieces. Draw a line 5/16" from the edge you just sawed, and cut the second wedge to that line. Cut the third wedge to reinforce the upper ends of the ¼" pieces, as shown in photo 20. Glue the two wedges in place.

12 Cut one end of each vault blank square by propping it against a stop on the table saw's miter gauge. The stop should be adjusted to hold the vault blank flat on the table where you're cutting it.

13 Place each blank on the vaulting jig, with the trimmed end of the blank tight against the lip on the bottom of the jig, and trace the jig sides onto the blank. To extend the planes of the jig sides accurately onto the blank, hold your pencil near its point while tracing.

14 With its table set at 22.5°, use the band saw to cut just outside the traced lines. During these cuts, the waste will always be below the blade. You can also trim the waste from the blanks using a dozuki saw (see page 10), with the blank held against the jig to establish the angle of cut.

15 Use the vaulting jig to help trim the vaults to size. In photo 21, I'm planing a side edge of the vault even with the side of the jig. The sides of the jig help establish the proper angle for trimming the sides of the vaults to the traced lines. The angle is more important, at this point, than the width of the vault. Make sure you plane the right edge of the vault even with the right side of the jig, and that the bottom edge of the vault remains tight against the lip of the jig while you do so. And be careful not to plane into the jig itself!

16 When you've trimmed the sides of the vaults, use the jig to cut the tops of the vaults to their 7" heights on the table saw (see photo 22). Add the thickness of the bottom of the jig to 7", and set the rip fence that distance from the blade. Hold the bottom of the jig snug against the rip fence.

BRUNELLESCHI'S BREAKTHROUGH

PHOTO COURTESY OF A PERFECT EXPOSURE, COLORADO SPRINGS, CO

THE FLORENCE CATHEDRAL—THE FOURTH largest cathedral in the world—was begun in 1296 by Arnolfo di Cambio, but was not consecrated until 1436. During more than 100 years of the cathedral's construction, no one knew how the dome could be built. Its basic shape had been established by the mid-fourteenth century, but its size and its height above the floor seemed to require extremely complicated—and ruinously expensive—scaffolding. By 1413, an octagonal drum, 14 feet thick, had been completed to support the dome, but even a competition in 1418 among the most accomplished architects failed to produce an acceptable plan for its construction.

Within months, Filippo Brunelleschi—who at 24 was a member of the Silk Guild, a sculptor, a painter, and a goldsmith, but not an architect—presented a model and a plan for an innovative construction technique. His plan called for building two brick domes, one inside the other, connected by a web of ribs and encircling bands. While impressed enough to pay Brunelleschi for his model, the building committee was reluctant to entrust the dome to an untested architect. They required Brunelleschi to work with Lorenzo Ghiberti, the sculptor to whom he had finished second in the competition for the doors of the Baptistry, and they assigned Battista d'Antonio as master of the works, or structural engineer. Brunelleschi accepted this arrangement, then feigned an illness that prevented him from working until the committee realized that Ghiberti was incapable of carrying out the construction. Brunelleschi supervised all aspects of the dome's erection until it was completed in 1436. He then designed its marble lantern, which was installed shortly after his death in 1446.

Brunelleschi's innovation stemmed from two insights. First, he realized that concentric rings would keep the dome from deforming, much as barrel hoops keep the staves of a barrel together. He provided such rings by installing six concentric hoops between the layers of the dome, each hoop made of sandstone blocks with an iron chain pulled tight to their outside surfaces. Second, he knew that each layer of masonry in a dome formed a keystone that stabilized the layers below it. If all the bricks in each layer could be installed simultaneously, they would stay put; but, of course, that is impossible in practice. So Brunelleschi devised a way to tie each new layer incrementally to the previous layers. Using bricks four times as long as they were thick, he laid one brick vertically and three horizontally in a herringbone pattern. The vertical bricks tied each new course to three installed courses, so that only three bricks needed to be laid at once to achieve the keystone effect. This allowed both the bricks and the ribs to be built from the base octagon to the top octagon supporting the lantern, all without a supporting scaffold. Brunelleschi followed the implications of these two insights to design a complicated structure so strong that no cracks have appeared in the dome since its original interior frescos were painted.

PHOTO 23

PHOTO 24

PHOTO 25

ASSEMBLING THE DOME

1 Glue the right edge of each vault to a rib, as shown in photo 23, matching the inside curves and the bottom ends. There's no way to clamp this joint that I know of, so just hold the vault in place until the glue begins to set.

2 Hold a vault/rib in place on top of the octagon to see how much of the inner walls needs to be trimmed to allow the outside surfaces of the vaults to lie flush with the outer walls. Trim the inner walls with a low-angle block plane and a sharp chisel. In photo 24, I'm chiseling the corner between two inner walls to make way for a rib.

3 Now hold two vaults opposite each other on top of the walls, and, with your third hand, put the lantern on top of the vaults and between the ribs. The top of each rib should land in the center of a side of the lantern. Glue those two vaults to the walls, as shown in photo 25. Don't glue the lantern yet because you'll need to move it while you fit the remaining vaults.

4 Next, add two more vaults at right angles to the first two. Now you have four open spaces to fill. Try each new vault in turn, trim it if necessary, and glue it to the walls and the adjoining rib. You may want to fit all three vaults on one side before you glue them. Make sure that the tops of the vaults form a flat surface for the bottom of the lantern. Finally, glue the lantern in place. That wasn't so bad, was it?

PAINTING THE DUOMO

1 The Duomo was made of marble, stone, and brick, and you will probably want to use the colors of those materials, as represented in the photograph on page 127. Make sure that you prime and sand the house before painting it.

2 To make your wren house look even more true-to-life, add the rectangular decoration to the walls, as shown in the photo of the real Duomo.

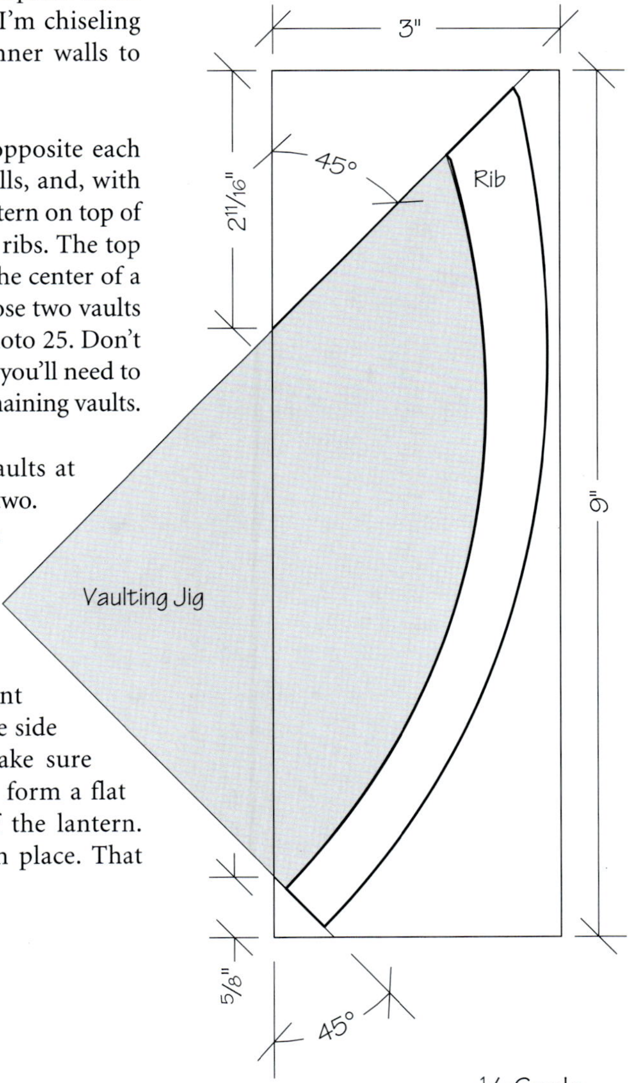

FIGURE 5. **Rib Pattern**

BIRDHOUSE DIMENSIONS

WILD BIRD SPECIES	FLOOR SIZE	BOX HEIGHT	ENTRANCE ABOVE FLOOR	ENTRANCE HOLE	HEIGHT ABOVE GROUND OR WATER	PREFERRED HABITAT CODES
American Robin*	7"x 8"	8 "	——	——	6–15'	7
	6"x 8"	8"	2"	2"	6–15'	7
Barn Owls	10"x 18"	15–18"	4"	6"	12–18'	4
Bluebirds	5"x 5"	8–12"	6–10"	1½"**	4–6'	1
Chickadees	4"x 4"	8–10"	6–8"	1⅛"	4–15'	2
Common & Northern Flicker	7"x 7"	16–18"	14–16"	2½"	6–20'	1, 2
Flycatchers	6"x 6"	8–12"	6–10"	1½–1¾"	5–15'	1, 6
House Finch	6"x 6"	6"	4"	2"	8–12'	7
House Sparrows	4"x 4"–5"x 5"	9–12"	6–7"	1³⁄₁₆–2"	8–12'	7
Nuthatches	4"x 4"	8–10"	6–8"	1¼–1⅜"	5–15'	2
Phoebes*	6"x 6"	6"	——	——	8–12'	7, 8
	6"x 6"	6"	2"	2"	8–12'	7, 8
Purple Martins	6"x 6"	6"	1–2"	1¾"–2¼"	10–15'	1
Downy Woodpecker	4" x 4"	8–10"	6–8"	1¼"	5–15'	2
Hairy Woodpecker	6" x 6"	12–15"	9–12"	1½"	8–20'	2
Pileated Woodpecker	8" x 8"	16–24"	12–20"	3 x 4"	15–25'	2
Red-Bellied Woodpecker	6" x 6"	12–15"	9–12"	2½"	10–20'	2
Red-Headed Woodpecker	6" x 6"	12–15"	9–12"	2"	10–20'	2

WILD BIRD SPECIES	FLOOR SIZE	BOX HEIGHT	ENTRANCE ABOVE FLOOR	ENTRANCE HOLE	HEIGHT ABOVE GROUND OR WATER	PREFERRED HABITAT CODES
Screech Owls	8"x 8"	12–15"	9–12"	3"	10–30'	2
Barn Swallows*	6"x 6"	6"	——	——	8–12'	7, 8
	6"x 6"	6"	2"	2"	8–12'	7, 8
Violet-Green and Tree Swallows	5"x 5"	6–8"	4–6"	1½"**	5–15'	1
Titmice	4"x 4"	10–12"	6–10"	1¼"	5–15'	2, 7
Prothonotary Warbler	5"x 5"	6"	4–5"	1⅛"	4–8', 3W'	3, 5
Wood Ducks	10"x 18"	10–24"	12–16"	4"	10–20', 6W'	3, 5
Wrens	4"x 4"	6–8"	4–6"	1–1½"**	5–10'	2, 7
Yellow-Bellied Sapsucker	5"x 5"	12–15"	9–12"	1½"	10–20'	2,4
Saw-Whet Owl	6 x 6	10–12"	8–10"	2½"	12–20'	1

NOTES

* These birds often prefer an open side instead of an entrance hole.

** Precise measurements required; if diameter is over 1½", starlings may usurp the nesting box.

PREFERRED HABITAT CODES

1. Open areas in the sun (particularly not shaded by trees), pastures, fields, or golf courses
2. Woodland clearings or the edge of woods
3. Above water or, if on land, with the entrance facing water
4. On the trunk of a large tree, or high in little-frequented parts of barns, silos, water towers, or church steeples
5. Moist forest bottomlands, flooded river valleys, or swamps
6. Semi-arid country, deserts, dry open woods, and edges of woods
7. Backyards, near buildings
8. Near water; under bridges, barns

FINISHING

You have many options for finishing your birdhouse, depending on the degree of detail you want to include and the amount of weather-resistance you need. In most of the projects pictured, I chose a middle path between simplicity and detail, evoking the features that help distinguish each style. The following sections provide general painting instructions and an innovative method of achieving a high level of detail, especially for decorative houses.

PAINTING YOUR HOUSE

You can use any exterior paint or artist acrylics to finish the house, but be aware that some birds, like some humans, avoid paint odors. Therefore, leave the inside of your house unpainted, and use latex in preference to alkyd paint.

As always with woodworking, the most important ingredient of a good finish is doing a good job of sanding. Fortunately, you need go no higher than 150 grit to smooth your birdhouse enough for paint. Prime all the exposed surfaces, paying special attention to the plywood edges. It's best to apply two coats to those edges to help seal the end grain. Sanding between coats will help smooth the raised grain, too. You can use any exterior paint or artist acrylics to finish the house. You won't need much, so maybe those half-empty cans in the garage (or in your neighbor's) will come in handy. With proper planning and masking, many of these projects lend themselves to spray painting.

Some of the birdhouses will be difficult to paint after they're fully assembled. Keep this in mind while you're building, and paint those areas now that will be hard to reach later. But don't get any primer or paint on the places which will need glue. For example, you might paint the eaves and roof edges before you attach the roof. Then assemble, fill your nail holes, prime, and paint the roof.

Painting these projects involves plenty of "cutting in," or painting with a new color right next to another color. You can make this process faster and more accurate by using masking tape to cover the paint already in place. Masking is a great way of painting windows, too. Say that

you're painting a yellow house with white trim. First, paint the house yellow. Then mark the area of window glass everywhere inside the window trim, and paint it a medium gray, making sure the edge of the gray ends inside the trim area. When the gray paint has dried, you can use wide masking tape to cover the entire area of the window, its trim, and at least ½" past the trim. Draw the window trim, including muntins and mullions, on the masking tape. Using a thin-blade craft knife and a clear ruler, cut on those lines, and remove all the trim areas. Paint your white trim color, then remove the masking tape as soon as you're done painting.

USING PRINTED DECORATION

In two cases, the Cape Cod Bluebird House (see page 29) and the Saltbox Wren House (see below and page 16), I experimented with applying printed paper house sides to achieve a realistic appearance. I designed the sides on the computer, using a modelling and rendering application, and printed them on photo paper with an inkjet printer. You could use any graphics application to draw the clapboard siding, windows, and trim. Define your clapboards with wide grey lines to simulate shadows. And make the print slightly larger than its wall, so you have room to trim. The water-soluble ink does not adhere particularly well to glossy paper, so you must handle the prints carefully. The following instructions at right tell how to apply your printed sides, but be sure to do so before you add the roof or any other trim to your house.

1 Sand the house and prime it, then sand again.

2 Mask all of the house except for two opposite sides, the front and back of the CapeCod Saltbox, for instance. You can use wide masking tape to cover everything, including bridging over the roof, or cover most of the house with paper, taping only the edges. Be particularly careful to keep adhesive out of the nesting cavity.

3 To eliminate half of the problem of aligning the printed side, you should cut only its bottom edge, as follows: Put the house on a scrap of plywood on a clean surface. Trim the bottom edge of your print so that the image portion aligns with the house when you rest the bottom edge of the print on the table.

4 Prepare a separate space, preferably outdoors, with a plastic sheet backdrop, in which to spray the house and the two prints. Put the prints, face down, on some newspaper. Use a high-quality, permanent spray adhesive, available at art-supply stores. Follow the directions on the can for a lasting bond. Spray the two opposite house sides and the two prints.

5 Carrying the house back to the scrap plywood and fetching the two prints will probably allow enough time to pass for a good bond. Don't let the print touch the side until you're sure you have it aligned properly. See photo 1, in which I am applying the first side. Turn the house, and press the other side in place.

PHOTO 1

PHOTO 2

6 Lay the house, first side down, on some clean paper. With another piece of paper over the second side, press the print down firmly. Then turn the house over to do the same everywhere on the first side. Trim each side with a narrow-bladed craft knife, as I'm doing to the fourth side in photo 2.

7 Apply at least two coats of satin or gloss polyurethane to the first two sides, allowing plenty of drying time between coats.

8 Before you apply sides three and four, make sure that the edges of the first two printed sides are trimmed flush with the unfinished sides. Then mask the first two sides, as shown in photo 2. Use masking tape that's not very sticky, and reduce its tack further by pressing each piece against your shirt just before you press it in place. The masking tape can lift the ink from its paper, so allow as little tape as possible to touch the prints.

9 Apply the third and fourth sides as before, and remove the masking tape as soon as you can. Finish those sides with two coats of polyurethane, as before, but be sure to cover the trimmed edges of the third and fourth sides, too. Then you can finish assembling the house. Before the final assembly, you'll want to paint any pieces that will contact the printed sides.

MOUNTING AND MAINTENENCE

FALL CLEANUP

If your birdhouse becomes infested with insects, try a thorough cleaning first. If the bugs return, you'll have to proceed to chemical warfare, but be sure the insecticide you choose will not harm birds. Deter wasps by coating the inside of the house with cented bar soap.

When the weather turns cold, your birds will have left the house for you to clean up after them. Ungrateful brats. Oops! I forgot—they're your birds. All the houses in this book have provisions for cleaning, so find the screwdriver, a stiff brush, and a bucket of soapy water. Get rid of all the nesting material, and scrub the inside of the house until it sparkles (in your eyes, of course). Be sure to rinse thoroughly. That's it—you're ready for another family next spring.

PUTTING IT UP

First, decide where to put your birdhouse. The chart on page 136 suggests some preferred habitats for particular species, and your yard may limit your choices as well. The chart also indicates the height at which particular houses should be mounted. Be sure that your house is at least 5' above the ground, as a first deterrent to predators. Squirrels and raccoons like to eat bird eggs and hatchlings. Squirrels can jump amazing distances, so situate the house well away from overhanging branches. Smearing axle grease on the pole may help deter nasty rodents, but a metal or plastic cone at least 20" in diameter, attached around the pole, offers a strong defense. Hanging a similar cone above a suspended feeder will help keep squirrels from helping themselves.

A threaded, galvanized pipe offers the most direct way of mounting your birdhouse on a pole. Screw a matching threaded flange to the bottom of the house. Then sink the pipe at least 18" in the ground, embedded in a suitable foundation, and you're all set. Alternatively, you can mount your house on a wooden 3 x 3. Cut a piece of plywood to a 6" square, and screw it to the top of the post. Then screw upward through the overhanging plywood and into the bottom of the house.

METRIC CONVERSION TABLE

INCHES	CENTIMETERS	INCHES	CENTIMETERS
⅛	3 mm	12	30
¼	6 mm	13	32.5
⅜	9 mm	14	35
½	1.3	15	37.5
⅝	1.6	16	40
¾	1.9	17	42.5
⅞	2.2	18	45
1	2.5	19	47.5
1¼	3.1	20	50
1½	3.8	21	52.5
1¾	4.4	22	55
2	5	23	57.5
2½	6.25	24	60
3	7.5	25	62.5
3½	8.8	26	65
4	10	27	67.5
4½	11.3	28	70
5	12.5	29	72.5
5½	13.8	30	75
6	15	31	77.5
7	17.5	32	80
8	20	33	82.5
9	22.5	34	85
10	25	35	87.5
11	27.5	36	90

INDEX